Praise for Dreams Never Die

"Troutman has captivated me with this exciting read. This book is an excellent guide for dreamers who desire to become doers."

Toya Prayer, Entrepreneur

"Dreams Never Die is a brilliant book! Troutman did an amazing job at making this book an easy read, while inspiring all who will read it."

Raymond Brunner, CEO, Community Powerhouse Energy'

"This book is a must-have in your collection. It offers loads of information on how to achieve and maintain success. Troutman's story is truly incredible."

George B. Harrison, Jr., CEO, GBH Photography

"I've read many books about success principles, but nothing compares to the impact prosperous business owners who are willing to share their stories of both struggle and triumph have on us all. This book is a wonderful reminder that we should not give up on our dreams. They are attainable."

Nicole Young, Entrepreneur

Dreams Never Die

Clement T. Troutman

Troutman Alliance, LLC
Maryland

Dreams Never Die
by Clement Troutman
Published 2021 by Troutman Alliance, LLC
Odenton, Maryland

©2021 by Clement Troutman

All rights reserved. No part of this book may be reproduced or transmitted in any form whatsoever without permission from the author except in the case of brief quotations embodied in articles, reviews, or books.

First Edition Published by Troutman Alliance, LLC

Printed in the United States of America
1 2 3 4 5 6 7 8 9 0

ISBN-13: 978-1-7373767-0-5 (paperback)
eISBN: 978-1-7373767-1-2

Library of Congress Control Number: 2021914220

Editor: Ayanna Moo-Young (mybooksupport.com)
Cover Designer: Edward Holton (g3mini-graphix.com)

This book is dedicated to the loving memory of my parents Clemmie and Betty Troutman, my wife, Jackie, and my children Jocelyn, Jordan, and Ashanti. Never forget you are God's greatest creation and with you in my life, I live my dreams every day!

ACKNOWLEDGEMENTS

Writing a book was more challenging than I thought and yet more rewarding than I could have ever imagined. None of this would have been possible without God and my wife and best friend, Jackie. Thank you for your patience and encouragement throughout this journey and holding down our family while I dedicated countless hours to writing and editing. Always remember that there is no me without you.

To my children, Ashanti, Jocelyn, and Jordan, you are my inspiration for everything I do. Thank you for showing me how to be the best person and Dad I can be. You are my greatest gift from God and ultimate accomplishments of my life. You are the pilot lights of my heart.

I am eternally grateful to my siblings and their families: John & Wanda, Leon, Glen & Toni and Glenda & Darlene, their children, Danielle, Justin, Marcus Tor, and DaSheem, my dear aunts, Frances and Clarice, and my cousin Damon. You continue to inspire me to keep moving forward with your love and strength of family.

To Jerry Anderson and Ray Patterson, you were my first friends I made when I moved to Macon, Georgia from Detroit. You stood by me during every struggle and all my early successes. Together we dreamed and believed we were champions, even in the projects of Tindall Heights. We were then, and we still are today. Thank you for taking me in as a friend for life.

To my dear friends, Mike & Norma Gold, who mentored me over the years, I thank you for being a friend I could depend on, who through your example showed me what it takes to be a servant leader.

To Jack & Magee Spencer, my rich dad, who dedicated his life to serving others, and always reminded me that I mattered. Magee, we love you, and Jack (RIP) will never be forgotten.

To my former IT Engineering colleagues, Jim & Elaine Dingledine, Tammy Turpin, Phyllis King, Candace Cook, Charlene Johnson, Mike Newman, Tom MacNamara, Yolande Pickens, Rob Smith, Jaronda Perry, Terry Grimes, and Brian Glenn, thank you for your support and friendships as we collectively protected our systems networks, while at the same time hosting birthday, Christmas, and Halloween parties. Our time together was truly a special time, not just for the work but for the friendships that remain.

Writing a book about the story of your life is a humbling process. I am forever indebted to my former Navy colleagues, Mike Bruton, Don Bossett, Rob Smith, Shelton Rainey, Leonard Caver, Lenny Reese, and Alex A. Miller. You have all impacted my life at different stages of my life through the years and I thank you for being honorable men of character and valor I could learn from then and now.

David Stansbury, Leo Nwadibia, Gene Tolbert, and David Magby, you represent the gateway to the development of tomorrow's new business leaders, and I am thankful that you had the courage to step out on faith to claim your business dreams, and by doing so, created opportunities for others to do the same. Thank you for always dreaming big.

Gene Brodie (RIP), David Cape, Roy McWilliams, Jesse Anthony and all my fellow 1975 State Champion brothers of Central High "BigOrange" Charger's football, thank you for creating a winning legacy that has endured and remains unblemished.

Keith Singletary and Darrell Spears, your leadership, advice, and support to our business as we opened in the community of Capitol Heights was vital to our success and growth that first year. You helped us navigate many unknowns which ensured our business growth from day one and I thank you.

Gary Michael, thank you for your support and trust in our vision to serve healthier food options throughout the Prince George's County to needed families, first-responders, and essential workers. Serving on the Board of The Mission of Love Charities, Inc. with you and our winning team is an honor and privilege.

To all great friends and colleagues (which are too many to name) that God has placed in my life over the years, I have truly been blessed to know you.

To all the members of The Tropical Smoothie Café Dream Team of Capitol Heights, both old and new, thank you for believing we could serve on a higher level. Your dedication to hard work and commitment to finish has improved the quality of life for over 1 million and counting.

Finally, I thank my coach, Author Ayanna Moo-Young, for your guidance, incredible patience, and direction every step of the way. I have learned so much on what it takes to write in an entirely new, exciting, and meaningful way.

Contents

Preface vii
Introduction ix
1. Why vs. How: The Early Years 1
2. An Ode to Betty Joe 13
3. Vison vs. Sight 21
4. Decide: Tell it In Advance 27
5. Heart vs Mind Power 47
6. Fear vs. Faith 51
7. Failing Forward 65
8. Ridicule vs. Reward 75
9. Change is Inevitable 87
10. Success: A Common Language 93
11. Perseverance: A Made-up Mind 99
12. Success: A Winning Thought Process 123
13. The Power of Self-love 137
About the Author 157

PREFACE

It's important to continually pursue our dreams, and you have everything you need to get what you really want out of life. In this book, you will learn how to identify and move past obstacles that stand between you and your dreams and confirm you can have them. The resources mentioned are the result of personal experiences, coupled with inspirational readings and attending seminars on success for 10 years to better understand why some achieve significant levels of success while others do not.

Dreams Never Die was born after I retired from being a DoD Contractor on my birthday in 2017 and went into business for myself, achieving a lifelong dream. This book is written to remind all dreamers that it's never too late. Whether in pursuit of a new dream or an old one that came up short, this book is for you. It was created to help the underdog and anyone willing to strive to reach their full potential. To fully benefit, read this book in its entirety the first time, then read it a second time to fully grasp the content.

INTRODUCTION

We all dream. We dream of having better jobs and lifestyles, being in greater financial positions, having flourishing relationships and impeccable health. We are all striving for something. And although we have had obstacles to overcome during our lives, despite these setbacks, we reach our goals. Maybe you wanted to achieve something as a child that required hard work, effort and commitment such as, to be the creator the number one science project, to be selected for the school play or to start on the basketball team. Repeatedly, we've faced challenges, overcame them, and succeeded because we trusted ourselves. Yet, despite our accomplishments, we continue to second guess our abilities to achieve success in the future. Why do we stop trusting ourselves and our grind? We've simply forgotten.

Dreams never expire, people do. During an interview on the podcast, "Tell Me About the Hard Part", I was asked: "What motivates you to keep going at this stage of your life when it comes to your business success?" My response was simply, "Dreams never die!" I went on to explain that our dreams are long-term ideas and personal gifts from God, given exclusively to us in the form of unexplainable thoughts and visions that go far beyond our current capacities.

As a child, I believed anything was possible. I had no doubt, fear, or other barriers. If you were anything like me, you also believed you could be whatever you wanted. And guess what? You were right, and you still can! You must first, however, gain an understanding of what happened between yesterday and today that caused you to change how you perceive your dreams. Why do those things we believed were possible as children seem so challenging today? The answer is simply, *conditioning*.

What is right and what is wrong? What is acceptable and unacceptable? What is good versus what is bad? Since childhood, we have all been receiving subliminal information – most negative to some degree – impressing upon our subconscious minds of what we now consider impossible, instead of what is. This conditioning, although not intended to be negative, helps shape how we view the world from a safe, cautious perspective. Our minds possess the most powerful computing power on the planet, and the programming entered will determine what comes out. Thus, the computer programming phrase: *garbage in, garbage out*. Most think programming begins at birth, but it begins much sooner. Our brains consume and record information continuously, starting with our environments. Babies begin the learning process while in their mother's womb. What a mother thinks during and after pregnancy impacts her child. If she has a positive outlook on life, chances are high the child will also. To the contrary, if she has a negative and bleak outlook about the future, the child will most likely mirror this behavior, too. Wouldn't it be great if doctors prescribed positive reading materials for expectant mothers to read to their unborn children? Ken Blanchard, in his book, *Whale Done*, highlights how people are not conditioned to focus on the things we do well, but just the opposite. And when I read it, I immediately began to examine how this statement applied to my own family. I don't recall moments in which Jackie and I purposefully provided feedback to our children when they were playing well together, but rather when they were not. We – or at least I – unknowingly focused on what was going wrong and needed to be corrected rather than what our children, Jocelyn and Jordan, were doing right. No wonder it's so difficult to think positively about our dreams. Many of us have been conditioned to focus on not achieving them instead of succeeding.

Children are further conditioned through the educational system, continuing the pattern of limited thinking and what appears to be far-fetched possibilities. The American education system has come under a lot of scrutiny lately for their programs or lack thereof. The system follows a specific learning criterion where students are taught key job skills; however, learning how to start a business is not a normal component of what is taught. Most high school and college curricula focus on the management aspect of business rather than ownership. There is no Dreams 101 class offered to my knowledge. Therefore, when you have a dream and you decide to go after it, it may conflict with the ideals of those who are not entrepreneurs. However, the free enterprise system is alive and well in America! Day in and day out, immigrants get sworn into becoming American citizens, leaving their native countries for a chance at the American Dream. The fact that they have an opportunity to start a business of their own and take care of their families both here and abroad makes the sacrifice well worth it. Embrace the idea that there is always another level of possibilities you can tap into through the power of your dreams.

"You Become What You Think About, All Day Long!
~ Earl Nightingale

Imagine how different life would be if we could adjust our thinking to only accept positive outcomes. You asked a date to the high school prom and they said, "Yes." The loan for your dream home, approved. The ideal business contract opportunity was awarded to you despite the existence of many other competing businesses. For every one of these examples there is also potential for a negative outcome. If you focus on the positive, you will find that in most cases the negative outcome never existed. Focus on what you want and not what you don't want. Expect a positive result and you will get one. Remember to view your dreams as you did as a child. Believe they are possible. Imagine not being able to fail. What would be your next move?

CHAPTER ONE
Why vs. How: The Early Years

"My life is my message" ~ *Mahatma Ghandi*

I was born in Detroit, Michigan in the 1950's. My father was a laborer in the construction industry, while my mother was a stay-at-home mom. My older sister Mary and four younger siblings – John, Leon, Glen and Glenda (the twins) – rounded out our family. Life as I knew it was good. I lived in the mecca of soul music, Motown, and can recall images of popular musical groups and artists such as the Supremes, Temptations, Jackson Five, Aretha Franklin, Stevie Wonder and

Marvin Gaye. There was a booming automotive industry and everyone appeared to be living the good life. We lived in an urban community where homeownership was prevalent and every family seemed to have a car. Some even had boats that could be seen on the Detroit River on weekends. These are all examples of what I saw as success and possibility. Our parents and other family members had migrated from Macon, Georgia in the early 1950's during *The Great Migration* (1916-1970), a movement in which many Black southerners moved to the Northeast and Midwest in search of work opportunities in the industrious Motor City. Ironically, my parents did not know each other at the time but eventually met at my great aunt's restaurant located on Detroit's west side.

Early on, I was an entrepreneur at heart and always kept a business of some sort. My very first business was collecting empty Coke bottles and redeeming them for 5 cents each. Another was shoveling snow from sidewalks for a dollar. I also had a lawn mowing business but only mowed on weekends because the push mowers of the 60s did not have engines, making grass-cutting an all-day event. These ventures were all profit with no overhead. They only required effort and sweat, of which I had plenty. I started my first official business at the age of 11 as a paper boy for the Detroit News. I was so proud. Pulling my shiny red wagon with Detroit News branded on the side, I delivered newspapers to 60 customers after school each day. I considered myself a big deal. Things were normal and easy in my world back then; however, they were rapidly changing for the worse.

My father was a good man when sober. The problem was those times were rare. He was in a personal fight for his life with a powerful enemy – alcohol – and losing. It quickly destroyed our safe and secure family environment, filled it with fear and uncertainty, and capped it with domestic violence. My mother, although small in stature, had the courage to fight for the family's well-being. She stood up to an oftentimes intoxicated husband who would consume the family's income drinking with so-called friends instead of coming home or buying food. When she challenged him, he would beat her. Eventually, Mary ran away and I became the oldest – the only child left in the home who was conscious enough to remember the unfortunate details, causing emotional scares I carry to this day.

My mother eventually separated from my father and since he was no longer around to protect us, she was forced to figure things out on her own. We lived in shelters and government programs sustained us. This was humbling, but at least we were safe. We received financial assistance from the Department of Social Services and were eventually placed in an apartment. I experienced many hungry nights and on Christmas mornings, there were no gifts to open. This was a lot to process for a black kid who had already seen evidence of a more prosperous life in the booming Motor City. The one question I could never answer during that time was, "Why me?"

Although everything appeared chaotic around us, we always had the support of our extended family, spearheaded by my mother's uncle Washington "Wash" Hutchings. He and his wife, Aunt Bessie, were well-respected members of the community, pastor and first lady of a local church. His brother, Uncle Minter "Sam" Hutchings Jr. and wife, Aunt Lee, were also influential. Wash and Sam were brothers of my deceased, maternal grandfather, Oscar Thomas Jr. They both had nice homes and luxury cars. They migrated to Detroit in the 1950's to take advantage of the booming automotive industry. They moved mom there at age 15, along with her grandmother, Tommie Thomas or Big Momma, as we affectionately called her. When Mom was 7 years old, Big Momma assumed custody of her because her mother, Willie Maude Cornelius Thomas, died in her late 20s. In 1971, Uncle Wash and Aunt Bessie offered to raise the twins to provide them a stable home environment. It wasn't an easy decision for Mom but she agreed to the arrangement, knowing they'd take great care of them. I experienced my first introduction to the South at that time. Mom moved back to Macon, Georgia with my brothers and I to live with Big Momma. I was only 13, but it was a major wakeup call. The uncertainty left me with the same looming question: "Why me?"

The value of growing up in Detroit prior to moving to Macon was immeasurable. The first thing I noticed was the major economic divide between the races. The nice houses were on what was referred to as the white side of town, while the old, broken-down homes were on what was referred to as the black side. Both races appeared content with this arrangement, but this was a major problem for me from the beginning. I had already been exposed to black homeowners living in nice communities and I could not understand why there was such a difference. However, seeing the City of Atlanta was similar to Detroit offered a little relief, as I previously thought the South was only made up of countryside living with farms and livestock.

We lived in the projects of Tindall Heights. I attended Miller's A and B Middle Schools before moving on to Central High School, an all-boys school. Ray and Jerry, who also lived there, were my new best friends. We dreamed of one day playing for the Central Chargers, the most dominate high school football team in middle Georgia. The team was founded on the success principles of discipline, teamwork, and commitment. Only the very committed made the team because the coaching staff was just as committed to weeding out the quitters. During my sophomore year, I did just that – I quit. I thought I should have been a starter but was assigned to carry the equipment for the seniors and play on the B-Team. Winners are never content with being benched. Besides, I was faster and stronger than most players but hardly got the recognition I thought I deserved. My Uncle Leon, a decorated Marine who attended my games when he could, was livid when he heard the news. He told me very simply, "You never win when you quit." A statement I've never forgotten. I learned a valuable lesson that year, "Quitters never win, and winners never quit."

I felt miserable watching the team practice from afar. My decision had placed me back on the outside looking in. The following season, I realized that if I was going to achieve my dream of playing, I was going to have to humble myself, be teachable, and learn to be part of a team. I worked my way back onto the team, although the coaches never once made it easy for me. When we completed team drills, I had to do more. There were so many lessons learned that year, but two I will remember forever. The first, you must prepare to win. You must prepare yourself both physically and emotionally. A sign posted on our practice field read, Fatigue Makes Cowards of Us All. But the second, biggest lesson I learned was there will always be a price for success, and it must be paid in full. I haven't quit anything else since. When I start something, I am committed to seeing it through.

If you have ever pursued anything worthwhile, you've probably wondered: "Why do I have to do so much more than everyone else just to get the same results ... study harder, get up earlier, or stay up later?" I've discovered very few people who have attained significant levels of success have done it without these same questions. The difference is not so much whether you're ready to get up earlier, study harder, practice longer, or go the extra mile; but are you *willing*?

Later that year, my friends and I went from dreaming of one day playing under the lights, to making those dreams our reality. We had a disappointing season my junior year, but as seniors went on to win the state championship. Our record still stands today, 45 years later.

> *"Behind every seed of adversity, there is a seed of equal or greater benefit!" ~ Napoleon Hill*

In retrospect, I realize a challenging upbringing can be one of your greatest assets. I always felt there had to be a rest of the story. After witnessing a different way of life in the Motor City, there was something greater deep inside drove me and would not allow me give up. God had planted a seed of hope in my heart that would not be denied. No matter how dire the circumstances seemed, pain and disappointment fueled my determination to try even harder. "This underdog will have his day", I would tell myself.

I have always wanted to feel successful, admired and respected for doing something meaningful. I believe we all have a desire to make a difference in some way. Maslow defines self-actualization, or man's purpose for living as "to reach his or her full potential and the epitome of human existence". The fire deep inside me gave me hope that someday things would get better. This book was written during the COVID-19 worldwide pandemic, one of the greatest examples of hope in our existence. Every seed of adversity I've ever experienced was necessary. They have made me stronger and even more determined to succeed.

"When the winds stop blowing in your sails, row!"

Over the years, I've learned no matter where you go or live around the world, winners always compete. Whether it be a sports competition in the Philippines, Spain, Guam, or Japan, or for career advancement and professional development, the drive to succeed and win remains constant. There is a little extra in us all that is never satisfied and looking to contend. After experiencing recurring shoulder injuries during my collegiate football career and afraid I'd end up in a dead-end warehouse job, at the age of 20, I joined the U.S. Navy. During boot camp, I was appointed the top recruit leadership position, Recruit Chief Petty Officer (RCPO). As RCPO for Training Unit 136, I was responsible for the training and development of 82 nervous peer recruits. Interestingly, leaders somehow find their way to the head of the line when leadership is needed, even when it's not their intention. As the saying goes, "The leader cannot sit still on a parked train for very long.

CHAPTER TWO
An Ode to Betty Joe

"If I have seen further than others, it is by standing on the shoulders of giants." ~ Isaac Newton

You can always tell the quality of a tree by the fruit it bears, and there are very few positive influences in a person's life stronger than that of a mother. Mine was Betty Joe. Considered the cornerstone of our family, she was a constant reminder to always move forward despite the odds. Like me, she was the eldest of four children. Born in Macon, Georgia in 1937, she immediately faced setbacks. Her father, Oscar Thomas, Jr. died when she was 2 years old; and she lost her mother, Willie Maude, at the age of 7.

Mom was part of a proud and confident family, which aided immensely in her confidence and belief. The Collins, my grandmother's side of the family, was spearheaded by my great grandfather, Joe Collins. And, the Thomas family, my grandfather's side, was spearheaded by my great grandmother, Tommie Thomas (aka Big Momma). Both were instrumental in providing a family environment for mom (aka Ma-Tane), her brothers Leon Thomas (aka Pa-Tane) and Donald, and her sister Frances. The families were indeed the gap fillers for their growth and development. Any family committed to raising additional children had to consider the economic impact. It was not uncommon for children to be separated or dispersed to different family members to help shoulder the financial burden, and ours was no different. Big Momma raised mom in Macon, while both Uncle Leon and Aunt Frances were raised in Cincinnati, Ohio by the Collins side of the family. Although they grew up in a warm, loving environment safe from harm, the separation without explanation was painful and would have long-term implications. My uncles and aunts, Rev. Dr. Martin Luther King, Jr., Muhammad Ali, and Coach Gene Brodie were all inspiring. But the most influential of all was Big Momma and my mother. They always reminded me that I mattered and could do something significant to make a difference. This gave me hope.

The memories I have of Big Momma are truly priceless. Watching her, I witnessed true character. Her reverence for God resonated throughout all our lives. Big Momma would make us stop whatever we were doing whenever there was a thunderstorm – no playing, television, or talking – nothing. We were all forced to take a nap during such times. It is fair to say we were not excited whenever thunderstorms came. Her love for God and family was her greatest legacy and has passed down through five generations, continuing to this day. She was all in when it came to family and totally committed to raising Betty Joe.

During the Great Migration, the Northeast corridor towards New York, and cities towards the Midwest such as Detroit, Chicago and Cleveland, were all growing due to the demand for increased manpower. The Collins side of the family ended up in Ohio, while the Thomas family migrated to Detroit. As a young girl, Mom lived a sheltered life because she experienced epileptic seizures and wasn't allowed to go far from Big Momma's care. Through it all, she never embraced a victim mentality. While in high school, she wanted to get out and test herself against the world, so she joined the track team. She kept it a secret from Big Momma, knowing she wouldn't have approved. Betty Joe's determination showed in everything she did. Whether looking for a job or ensuring we had clothes on our backs and food to eat, she did whatever was required. She made things happen, and that's what you're going to have to do to get what you want. Without a car, a job, or employable skills, she always found a way. When her welfare check was delivered on the first of the month, "check day", with just enough money to take the bus, she'd dress to go out the door and return hours later in a taxi loaded with food. These were important events when you lived in the projects of Tindall Heights. Mom had faith like none I've ever known, truly child-like. If you paid attention, you would notice her daily actions demonstrated her faith.

She never spoke in terms of anything being impossible or too late to accomplish and saw everyday as an opportunity to move forward. I watched my mother persevere time and time again.

"Nothing in this world can take the place of persistence. Talent will not: nothing is more common than unsuccessful men with talent. Genius will not; unrewarded genius is almost a proverb. Education will not: the world is full of educated derelicts. Persistence and determination alone are omnipotent." ~ President Calvin Coolidge

Betty Joe was persistent and consistent, always looking to improve. She finally landed a job with the assistance of a dear neighbor, Ms. Hawthorne, whose son Ulysses was also on the football team. Once she was gainfully employed, she returned the welfare check to the Department of Social Services, although they insisted it wasn't necessary because the funds had already been allocated. However, Mom was adamant about returning the check, which taught me the true importance of character and integrity. Michael Angelo, while painting the ceiling of the Sistine Chapel lying flat on his back for months in a dark, obscure corner area, was asked: "Why do you care to spend so much effort painting that corner? No one will ever know." He replied, "God will know." Without saying a word, Betty Joe gave the same reply with her actions.

When Ray and I joined the U.S. Navy at the age of 18, Mom struggled with the emotions of not wanting me to leave but wanting me to succeed. I was serving abroad in Spain, when 44-year-old Betty Joe encountered a new, unexpected challenge that changed our family forever. A stroke left her paralyzed on one side of her body. While going through rehabilitation, she neither expressed feelings of doubt, nor did she have a victim mentality. Her focus was consistently on getting back to a state of normalcy and independence. Betty Joe faced this health challenge with an attitude that simply asked, "What challenge?" Her drive and strength gave us confidence and hope that we, too, could make it. Every time I encountered a setback, I could refer to Mom's example of resiliency. She made us all stronger and her actions reminded us everything would be alright.

Over the years, Mom traveled back and forth between Maryland and Detroit, serving everywhere she went. In Detroit, she assisted with the care of Aunt Bessie, who had looked out for her many years earlier, and her sister and grandchildren. In Maryland, she helped my wife and I with the care of our children. Betty Joe had a servant's heart throughout and relished the opportunity to be closer and serve her family. Never giving up on education, Bettie Joe returned to school and was actively working on her GED. She had a small apartment in Annapolis, Maryland and was in the process of completing the curriculum when she encountered another challenge in 2007, a second stroke.

The second stroke impacted her ability to walk, and she had to resort to use of a wheelchair. Yet, day in and day out, she trained to make her body as strong as possible. She had an indelible impact on everyone she encountered including many friends in her apartment complex, church, and nursing home. Her positive outlook on life showed itself in everything she did, even playing bingo. She was considered the queen of bingo and won daily, mainly because of her attitude. She always believed she was supposed to win, and that's what all winners must do. As you pursue your life's work, you may not have the talent, money, or time. Yet, don't get discouraged or lose faith. Be willing to prepare yourself so when the opportunity arrives, you will have just enough to *catch the bus* to your dreams. During the journey, you will not know how all the parts are designed to come together. The only guarantee you'll ever have is that if you don't go forward, the dream may never materialize. If you feel safe in your career but deep inside want to know your full potential, remember: "If you don't go, it won't grow." Expect to win in everything you do, leaving nothing to chance. If you lose at something, speak victory every chance you get and say what I heard Betty Joe say repeatedly: "I'm on my way back!"

CHAPTER THREE
Vison vs. Sight

If you could see the future, how would you want it to look? It's a thought-provoking question that could shape our decision-making in an instant. John Maxwell in his book, *Today Matters*, wrote: "You can tell what a person will achieve in the future based on their daily agenda." What inspires your daily agenda? Better health? More happiness? More time with family? Our decisions are influenced not so much by what we see today, but what we envision for tomorrow, and it does not discriminate. Whether we envision better health now or worse health in the future, the vision will cause us to act. A person in great health now, who anticipates failing health in the future, might be more inclined to make healthier choices today. On the other hand, a healthy person who envisions better health tomorrow may not be as inspired to act now. The healthier person may be overconfident about their wellness until it starts to decline. The same logic could be applied to financing. Someone who believes they will have better finances in the future may not be so inclined to take the necessary action steps today, while someone who feels their job is in jeopardy tomorrow will start planning their next job opportunity a lot sooner. What we envision cannot be seen except through the heart or what I like to call, *heart sight*. You must believe it to see it, instead of seeing then believing.

"The only thing worse than being blind is having sight but no vision." ~ Helen Keller

Using images as reminders is an especially important part of the process, since our brain translates words and thoughts into images. If you were to close your eyes and hear the words blue elephant, your brain would immediately conjure up an image of a blue elephant, although you did not see the actual words. Find pictures or images to use as reminders of where you're going. If you're planning to lose 20 pounds by a certain date, find pictures and post them where they'll be visible reminders to help you maintain focus. It's not necessary to track your progress daily but establishing periodic intervals for review is valuable. By creating visions of your desired life, you'll be able to see your finish line. The power of imagination is an incredible force that follows neither a pre-existing plan nor guide. Think of all the inventions that wouldn't exist if their creators hadn't followed this logic. Dreamers such as Wright, Edison, Ford, Pasteur, Disney, Gates, Jobs, Franklin, Tubman, Douglas, Rockefeller, Walton, Marriott, Kroc, Obama, Winfrey, Gordy, Gandhi, King, Mandela, Hershey, Mars, Bezos, DeVos, Bell, Ali, Jordan, and countless others wouldn't have made their everlasting mark on the world. Their contributions have made the world a better place for all. They all had the power of imagination and were willing to pursue it without conceding to the voices of others. Today, you are the new visionary who will set the stage for the next big thing. How big will it be? You won't know until you pursue it. You will make the world a better place once you do.

"For as the heavens are higher than the earth, so are my ways higher than your ways, and my thoughts than your thoughts."
(Isaiah 55:9 KJV)

Our dreams are from God. Just knowing its origin is all you need because the vision will become clearer as you go. Since God is the originator, it stands to reason that he is always first in our hearts and thoughts. Whenever you encounter a dream, the first thought is usually, "It's possible." However, a negative thought usually immediately follows, causing you to question it. These negative thoughts are not from God. Be sure to listen to the thoughts originating from the heart. There is no doubt or fear there. Think back. Have you ever taken the time to do an inventory of your successes? Once you do, you'll find that almost everything you ever really wanted to achieve you somehow accomplished. Despite seemingly impossible odds, you passed that exam on the final try, secured that sales account when others could not, attended college despite financial disadvantages, etc. How so? You had the ability from the onset, even if you didn't know it. I define success as, the accomplishment of a worthwhile goal or dream. Earl Nightingale stated, "… it's the teacher that wanted to become a teacher or the housewife who dedicated her life to taking care of her family, and both are doing a good job of it!" Success is relative to each of us. If your goal is to be a truck driver and you are, you are successful.

Within you lies unlimited power for success. Your ability to tap into this power is the key between winning and losing. Sure, there are a select few who were born with incredible physical gifts such as professional athletes or entertainers; but you also have a unique, equally as powerful gift inside you the world has yet to discover. And once you unlock your inner power, your thought process for success will emerge. Once we can accept our own ability to gain success, we can then embrace the successes of others. And by embracing your uniqueness, you will unleash unmatched power that will benefit others. Don't delay!

"Hope deferred makes the heart sick." ~ Proverbs

CHAPTER FOUR
Decide: Tell it In Advance

I remember when we were teaching our son Jordan how to ride his bike and his mother was very concerned that he would hurt himself in the process. She agreed to go inside so we could have a little one-on-one discussion about this obstacle (he had fallen in the last 3 attempts). So, we had a discussion while he was sitting on his bike, and I challenged him to repeat the words "I can do it", as he pedaled his bike, and he accepted the challenge. As I pushed him to get the pedaling going, he continued to repeat the phrase, "I can do it", and I let go of the bike. Down the street he went under his own power, pedaling on his own while saying aloud he could do it. And he did! You see, by focusing on his proclamation, Jordan completely made the importance of balancing on the bike a secondary priority, and his subconscious mind took over. The only problem was I forgot to show him how to stop once he got going. That was an entirely different teaching session but, ultimately, he succeeded because of his willingness to speak it into existence. You must do the same to get what you want.

Your own words will always have the greatest influence on your beliefs. The most qualified person to determine what you are willing to do is the person looking back at you in the mirror. The Bible states, "The power of life and death are in the tongue." We get in life in direct proportion to what we speak. Far too often we spend most our energy and time speaking on the things we don't want instead of the things we do. We speak about having a headache or being tired, or back pain, etc., but is this what we really want? If what you say is what you get, then we need to be very careful of what we say. Words have enormous power! When we speak with conviction about what we want and put the right energy behind it, something happens within us and to those around us to start things moving in that exact direction. If you speak it long enough, it is bound to happen. What if we could speak what we really want, even without belief? What would it take to do such a thing? The one-word answer is *faith*. Once your faith in what you want is strong enough, you will speak what you really want. The primary method for exhibiting faith is, doing. So, by doing and speaking, you will initiate enormous power to capture your dreams.

The power of speaking without evidence will always be misunderstood. The majority will not believe without seeing first. But the few who are courageous enough to embrace its power will find themselves being remembered by all those who may have doubted in the beginning. There will be those who promised to be part of the team that will not be there once things get tough. Some may not even show up at all. Financial projections could fall short or development costs may exceed expectations. Natural unknowns are always possible such as flash floods, tornadoes, and snowstorms. We still go in knowing that we really don't know – we believe. Yes, there are risks. However, never compromise the end-goal. Anyone in the world of software development will tell you that having a back-door is a necessary element to perform software updates on new software. Yet having these back doors also create vulnerabilities that could be exploited by would-be hackers. While they may serve as a great backup, their very existence creates computer weaknesses, open to exploitation. When it comes to your goals and dreams, having a back-door implies you have not made a quality decision, but have left yourself open to doubt, uncertainty and, ultimately, fear. Thoughts such as, "What if it doesn't work?" "Suppose they laugh at my ideas?" "Just in case it doesn't work I'll ...," are all prime examples of back doors left open as a failsafe position. A back-door leaves room for self-doubt to creep into your plan and, once in place, takes focused effort to remove it. Going forward, make the quality decision not to leave a back-door. No need to go in and update your dream once you've decided because things will eventually fall in line along the way. Remember, there's no rear-view mirror when you run this race. Keep moving forward and don't look back. Instead of believing what you see is what you get, be willing to accept the fact that what you don't see is what you get! Just because you can't see it, doesn't mean it isn't there. Decide, never to compromise!

I've also found there has never been a more defeating word in our vocabulary than the word *can't*. It is a word I consider public enemy number one for dreamers. If you want your goals to be brought to a halt quickly, use the word and watch the results. You must be wary of its negative power over your belief. Unchecked, it will linger and grow into disbelief of enormous proportions. When in the pursuit of what you really want, make sure *can't* has no space to grow. The Little Engine That Could, believed it could. There's no such thing as can't to a dreamer!

While faith and fear cannot co-exist, dreams and doubts can. Although opposites, both are necessary. Doubts are not always negative signals. They are an indication we are changing emotionally as we pursue our dreams. Anxiety of a new unknown during the birth of a new venture can easily be misinterpreted as fear. These emotions, once understood, confirm that we are headed in the right direction through this unknown point to a new known. Doubts can be used as emotional growth status checkers that we are on our way. Once the unfamiliar becomes familiar, doubt and fear are replaced with experience and confidence, so just keep moving forward until a new, productive way of thinking becomes your primary thought process.

Most doubt and fear stem from the desire to be accepted. It is so strong that it causes us to make detrimental decisions. We remain quiet when it is time to speak and stay still when it is time to move. People get both married and divorced, committing to unhealthy relationships out of perceived obligations by society. Likewise, they stay in them due to accepted societal norms (aka the stick-it-out syndrome). Most guys are extremely nervous when asking a girl out on a date no matter how cool, calm and collected they may appear, and so are the girls. Furthermore, most people are willing to work any position except sales. Why are we so afraid of sales when the greatest profession in the history of the world is sales? It is certainly the most profitable. If you had a great idea that could help the whole world but were reluctant to tell anyone, your inaction might do more harm than good. Why don't we speak our minds more freely? At the end of the day, you must be willing to face one of the most powerful words to ever exist in the history of the world – No. Because of this simple two-letter word, many questions that should be asked are never asked. Most people purposefully seek out opportunities that will guarantee an affirmative response, since most people associate the word *no* with failure or rejection. They internalize a no response as if something is wrong with them. The student that has a great idea to present to the science teacher fails to speak up out of fear that the idea will be rejected. Consequently, they'd rather sit quietly and let the class discussions pass by without sharing valuable, innovative ideas. To get what you want in life, you're going to have to speak up.

Make your decision final and back it up daily. If repeated long enough, you'll create a highly productive habit. In his book, *The Master Key to Riches*, Napoleon Hill explains the *creative habit force*. In this context, habits are not broken but replaced with new ones. These new habits will be the key to reaching your goals. Too often we make decisions and end up abandoning them, especially when maintaining them becomes difficult or the results are not as timely as we would like. Make an all-in commitment. When someone parachutes from a plane, rides a rollercoaster or plunges from a high bridge with a bungee cord, a decision is made that is irreversible. In the 1500's, Spanish conquistador Hernando Cortez ordered his men to burn their ships once landed to fight, understanding that there was no turning back and either they would be victorious in war or perish. They were at a point of no return. To get what you really want, you must *burn the ships*.

Write down what you will do before you do it. This action step is the greatest sign of faith you could demonstrate, aside from speaking. Most people have problems with this step and are afraid of being judged based on either their present or past. However, the truth of the matter is that no one can predict your future but God. You possess all the power you need to achieve what you deem important in the future. Write it down and work for it. You'll create a contract or promise to yourself in the process. You'll have the opportunity to prove it later. There's no turning back. Start to envision your future. When opening a new restaurant, most owners envision only a small number of customers will come initially, and growth will occur within a year or so. But what if customers come in a massive surge on day one? Will you be ready for the growth?

How many visitors have you averaged today, this week, or this month? How many transactions were conducted? These are examples of how we captured our mini wins during our first year in business at the café. While the two are related, they provided different, extremely beneficial information which helped us decide to stay the course or to do more if we were significantly behind. While the number of visitors in the café will always be a major pulse in the evaluation process, a bigger one turned out to be the number of daily transactions. We discovered that many of our customers dine with us multiple times a day and week. These are examples of mini wins we celebrate with the team. They represent small acknowledgements that a larger, future success is imminent.

A good success plan stems from first having a solid *why*. It is the inspiration behind goals that lead to actual plans. It also represents an emotional, heart-felt state that is not logical in nature. A grandfather has difficulty giving up cigarettes. Instead of the doctor telling him he'll die if he doesn't stop smoking, she might suggest that if he plans to be around for his granddaughter's wedding, he needs to give up smoking. This approach is more inspiring to him because an emotional connection was made that will cause him to think about setting the goal and achieving it.

"Once you know why, you can figure out how."

Establish a deliberate plan for capturing your mini wins. If your goal is to lose 20 pounds and the scale shows only a one-pound loss after a week of steady exercise, celebrate the one pound. If you barely passed a school test with a "C," celebrate the "C." If you stop to capture these moments, they will feed into your overall success strategy. Be sure to review them periodically and speak about them aloud to yourself and others. By doing so, you confirm within your mind and heart that you are headed in the right direction.

Sometimes, we are propelled forward by the cheerleaders in our lives. In football and basketball, the role of the cheerleader is just as important as the game itself. They provide energy, optimism, and encouragement to everyone in attendance, from the players to the people in the stands. Everyone needs cheerleaders in life. Have you identified the cheerleaders in your inner circle? They are easily identifiable. Full of positive support, you know you can count on them when things are down. Be sure to do your inventory of this incredibly special and vital asset while on your journey. They'll be there to pick you up when things get tough, and constantly remind you that you have what it takes. They will also be the ones waiting for you when you cross the finish line.

"Dig your well before you're thirsty." – John McKay

Additionally, many people struggle to determine the right timing to pursue their dreams. I was one of them. I thought once I achieved a certain professional level or saved enough money it would be time. I have learned over the years, however, that there is absolutely no time like today. Truly, all you have is right now. Yesterday is gone and tomorrow has yet to arrive, so the present is all we have. I wrestled with the idea of whether to step out or wait for another tomorrow for years. Then, I experienced a major reality check. Our kids Jocelyn and Jordan had grown almost overnight, and Jackie and I had become empty nesters in an instant. Where'd the time go? What I realized more than ever was time had become of the essence and, subconsciously, I had developed a sense of urgency in my heart. It was time. What would you do if you knew you couldn't fail?

Would you delay your opportunity to start a successful business or to have more freedom and time with family? How about having better health? Expect to win in the beginning and you will find it to be the perfect time. No one knows when it will happen, but just know that it will happen. Get started.

There will never be a perfect time and you will never be totally ready. However, there is always a perfect time to be willing! Voluntarily make changes. It makes for a better experience than being forced by adversity. A great example of this is relationships. Relationships require investments of time, love, laughter, and admiration. When should you tell your spouse that you love him or her? Right before someone else does. The start time begins the minute you make a quality decision, and you are willing to pay the necessary price to achieve what it is you want. Successful people evaluate what is required and make decisions quickly. They seldom change their minds once a decision has been made. They are committed problem-solvers who look for solutions to what appears to be barriers to their dreams.

On the other hand, unsuccessful people are very reluctant to make quick decisions. They want all the answers up front and are fearful of how much effort and commitment might be required. Sadly, these same individuals who decide slowly are quick to give up once challenges to their achievement surface. Perhaps people tend to shy away from starting a business or pursuing their dreams due to a lack of injection capital. Financial capital will always be a factor, but the decision is more important. Once you decide and stand firm on your decision, methods for acquiring the capital will appear. There are many sources out there such as angel investors or silent partners who are always looking for great business opportunities to invest in. You may feel inclined to reduce the size of the dream due to limited financial resources. The brain deals in logic, but what does the heart say? Instead of shrinking your dreams to match limited resources, grow the size of the limited resources to match the dream. You can assemble a knowledgeable team with the necessary financial acumen to evaluate financial options available to you. If you are the most knowledgeable one in your group, get a new group!

There is no time limit on a dream other than the ones we allow others to place on it. Don't get discouraged when others can't see, believe, or understand your dream. It is a personal vision that was designed specifically for you to see. Whether your dream is to create financial and personal freedom, to leave a legacy for seven generations, or to make the world a better place by helping others, you are the author of your own book of life and how it ends is totally up to you. Our only true limits are the ones we place on ourselves. A person who lives to be 85 years of age has lived 31,025 days. No matter your current age, it's not a bad idea from time to time to ask yourself, "How many days do I have?" This, I consider the reality check question. John Maxwell in his book, *Today Matters*, points out the importance of having a daily agenda, which informs our future expectations. Most of us tend to base our future on our past experiences. While this is not always a bad thing, we must be mindful that historical information is not totally indicative of what we will do in the future. So, while the past can provide some useful insight of what we've done well, we need to remember that it also highlights what we did not do well. By pursuing our dreams daily, we automatically demonstrate faith. Putting our daily agenda to work is the ultimate proof of a quality decision. Remember, your actions speak louder than your words. Be willing to decide, then do! Keep in mind that there are many options available. If one way doesn't work, choose another. Just don't give up on the destination.

You might ask, "Suppose I really don't know what I would like to do?" If you find yourself asking this question, you are not alone. I asked myself many times, and still do. A success vehicle may not always be readily identifiable from the onset. Many have started ventures with one purpose in mind, only to find themselves succeeding with something totally different. Conrad Hilton of Hilton Hotels started out with the idea of banking but ended up in the hospitality business. John Marriott began with a root beer stand, branched into catering, then evolved into hotels, as well. What was common between them was a willingness to decide and get started. They also had a desire to serve as many as possible, building the necessary alliances to maximize growth. Whether in business or through philanthropic opportunities, the goal remained the same. The same opportunity awaits you today. Touch as many people as possible with your product or service in such a way that they will be inspired and gladly pay for it. Be willing to remain flexible in the *how* of your success journey, while never losing sight of your stable *why*.

"Anyone can count the seeds in an apple, but only God can count the number of apples in a seed."

After signing our franchise agreement on 31 December 2015, we attended our first franchisee convention in Orlando, Florida and met all the existing franchisees from around the country – a great networking opportunity. We learned so much about our new business by attending breakout seminars and networking with owners. The most exciting part of the convention was Awards Night, where top producing franchisees were recognized. Sitting there with our name badges labeled "Freshman Franchisee", we learned that awardees had reached million-dollar levels and beyond. Using the convention app, we submitted our goals for the coming year. The first goal Jackie and I listed was to be a million-dollar business, the second was to be listed in the Top 100 List, and third was to be recognized as Franchisee Rookies of the Year. After listing our goals, we simply hit the send button, submitting our goals to the CEO. Upon returning home, I also sent an email of our intended goals to our regional Franchise Business Leader support staff. This was in April 2016. We intended to accomplish these goals by the 2018 Convention.

"When opportunity comes, it's too late to prepare." - John Wooden

Prior to our grand opening, I ordered extra marketing materials in anticipation of doing more business than anyone ever imagined possible. I remember our marketing sales rep recommending we order the standard amount of 500 coupons. Instead, I ordered five thousand. I was prepared to win!

We opened our doors on February 24, 2017, and the rest of the year was truly historic. The following year, Jocelyn I returned to the business convention (Jackie nor Jordan were available to attend), where we were recognized for reaching the $1 million level, as we had predicted. However, we didn't stop there. We were also recognized as the brand's first-ever $2 million store. But we didn't stop there. We were also the 2017 Rookie of the Year Award recipients! God does nothing small. His dream for you will always be bigger than your own personal capacity. Forget looking to accomplish your dreams under your own power. Instead, embrace the reality that you have been entrusted with a great gift, the gift to dream. Go after it with everything you have. At the right time, God will step in and do the rest.

CHAPTER FIVE
Heart vs Mind Power

"People may not always remember what you said, but they will remember how you made them feel." –Maya Angelou

Why do our feelings matter so much? Throughout history, major world events have occurred due to matters of the heart. The stories of Sampson and Delilah, The Trojan War, and the honorable sacrifices of the world wars resulted from matters of the heart. Those men and women defied both logic and common sense to overcome impossible odds. If you ask five different people from five different countries what five things matter to them most, they'd probably respond, "Love for family, happiness, good food, security and respect." These five are common to every being on the planet and all five impact our feelings. The omission of any one could lead to serious problems, including wars.

In his book, *Skill with People*, Les Giblin notes: "People are 10,000 times more interested in themselves and not in you." Essentially, we think about ourselves and how we feel much more than we consider how others think and feel because our feelings about ourselves stem from the heart. Until we can validate our own importance, we are unable to fully accept the validation of others. And when we acknowledge the importance of others it creates harmony, cooperation, and agreement.

Offering is easier from a position of abundance, whether it be in money, food, education, or love. Ever notice how some people appear generous, giving, and forgiving than others? In most instances, if you look deeper into the person's background, you will find that their ability to offer or forgive is in direct proportion to the size of their ego or self-esteem. If one person was rewarded for doing a good job, chances are they are more confident and outgoing than others. With a full positive ego tank, they have more to give and share. Similarly, a person who did not receive recognition along the way will feel they do not have enough to give. But it's never too late. Look at your personal inventory and you will find you still have more than enough to offer. By offering the little you have, you'll have even more to give.

The price for serving can be a hefty one, but the more you serve the bigger the price tag. Talk to anyone who serves a lot of people whether in business, politics, entertainment or medicine, the price for the services they provide can be extensive. Not only monetarily but in time, physical labor, education, teambuilding, networking, and organization. Commitment grows exponentially with responsibility. It was Napoleon Hill that said; "From every seed of adversity, there is a seed of equal or greater benefit." There's a benefit right within your down moments that is most likely your greatest opportunity for success. Be willing to pay the full price for what you want, it's worth it. Remember: The price for life is sacrifice! People are most remembered not for what they received but for what they gave!" The Book of Mark states, "But those that were down on the good soil are the ones who hear the word and accept it and bear fruit, thirtyfold, and sixtyfold and hundredfold." You are the good soil! Give generously and welcome rejection when it appears. It confirms you are willing to serve others as a giver. Like the changing seasons, there will ups and downs along the way. However consistent commitment to what you want over time will yield results. Steady wins the race!

CHAPTER SIX
Fear vs. Faith

"The heart has its own reasons…" ~ Pascal

Although we grew up poor in Detroit and Georgia, we always believed things would get better tomorrow. I have come to learn that lacking financial resources doesn't necessarily mean you're poor in all aspects of life. Many have significant material resources but suffer from failed relationships or health challenges. An office executive could work 60-70 hours a week, get minimum sleep, eat processed foods, and seldom exercises but have a large bank account. Contrarily, a minimum wage earner could walk to work and get in at least 13,000 steps daily, eat vegetables regularly with little to no meat, and drink water daily.

Forty years later, the executive may use all his hard-earned money to satisfy major health issues; as, the laborer regularly saved his modest income over the years and now travels the world freely because of his superior investment decision to be rich in health.

When I was 12, I shoveled snow in wintertime to earn money. Most jobs paid no more than three dollars per house, a fortune back in the 1960's. One Saturday I had the opportunity of a lifetime, to shovel an entire gas station lot for twenty dollars. I had never seen that much money in my life! I jumped on the opportunity and worked all day to complete the job. It wasn't easy at all, but I did it and was rewarded as promised. I immediately gave ten dollars to my mother to help with groceries and was allowed to pocket the other ten. What enabled me to persevere despite falling temperatures and heavy snow was focusing on the reward at the end. Focus on your reward not the payment plan. Hope is also an extremely powerful emotion that lies within all of us. Where there is hope, there is no fear. Fear is replaced by faith. You must cling to hope as you pursue what you want. It is vitally important to maximize the opportunity before you, and when you have hope, you have more than you need to finish.

> *"Hope deferred makes the heart sick."* ~
> *Proverbs 13:12-14*

Living in Tindall Heights there was an area we called the horseshoe because of the shape of the street. Racing to see who was the fastest in the neighborhood was a big deal then, and the horseshoe was the designated proving ground. At nighttime, we'd meet under the streetlights and to race to see who was the fastest. The word about whomever won spread quickly around the neighborhood. When you set out to do something in a new environment, you're going to be tested. When you do, just be willing to run your race. By doing so, you will earn the respect of others who have run similar races.

When we believe in a certain outcome, we tend to get more of it. Let's say you are on top of a 10-story burning building and the bottom floors are on fire. Your only chance for safety is to jump 5-feet to an equally tall, adjacent building. Would you *try* or *do your best* to jump to safety; or would you make a quality decision and jump the 5-feet? Chances are you would jump 6 or 7 feet to be sure you'd make it. *Believing* is the first step.

What you believe you can do in your heart is a major factor in achievement, not what others believe. The Book of Mark states, "…all things are possible to him who believes." Taking deliberate action early in a process can have significant impact. Think back to your childhood. There are countless examples of the power of belief through action.

I remember my first experience in a swimming pool. I was an adult in Navy Boot Camp. The Navy has undeniably the finest swimmers in the world but unfortunately, I was not one of them. As recruits, we had to successfully pass the swim test or run the risk of being dismissed altogether. On the day of testing, Training Unit 136 was split into two groups, swimmers and non-swimmers. For the swimmers, the process was straight-forward. Dive off an 8-foot tall diving board and land down into a 12-foot deep pool, tread water for about 5-

minutes, swim the length of the pool, and you were done. However, there were 25 of us who were non-swimmers or "rocks" as we were known; and we were terrified.

Once the swimmers were done, all rocks had to get up on the diving board one-by-one and dive off into the pool below. There were professional swimmers in the pool standing by to assist just in case, but the fear we each experienced at that moment was very real. In fact, it was so strong that at least 5 recruits refused to follow the command to jump and were immediately processed for discharge because their fear was overwhelming and could have caused lives at sea.

The fear immediately dissipated once I stepped off the board. Thoughts that I might not be able to do it were replaced with immediate confidence that I could. My belief appeared instantly once I acted. Perhaps if those who refused to jump had just acted, they would have discovered they indeed could swim. Their indecision compounded their fears and worked adversely against their intended goals.

If you've ever mentioned your intentions to achieve unbelievable goals to others such as start a business, donate enormous sums of money to charity, travel the world, etc., you've most likely heard questions such as: How's your business going? Have you donated the money yet? ... When will you start traveling the world? These are examples of doubt questions, or queries of disbelief from people looking for proof that you achieved what you said you would do. Their lack of support for your vision doesn't mean that it is unattainable. They just can't see it yet and they will once you show them. While they don't have a right to judge you, they do have a right to look for evidence of truth. The Book of Luke (KJV): 6:43 states, "Wherefore you will know them by their fruit..." So, although they shouldn't judge you, they are within their rights to be fruit inspectors of truth.

Passion is the fuel that overcomes anxiety, doubt and fear. If you look back over your life, you will find that whatever drove you to achieve success, you were passionate about it. The things that we are passionate about we do. A basketball player constantly envisions the game of basketball. A rap artist writes down new lyrics while waiting in line to catch a flight. The photographer takes a photo while riding a metro train and it ends up in an art gallery. You stay up all night to catch a 3am flight for a vacation to Hawaii. These actions were all fueled by passions of the heart. When you focus on what's in your heart, it will feed your mind with the necessary energy it needs. All success starts in the heart, and it can override the odds!

I remember how frustrated I used to get when colleagues with whom I shared my dreams of retiring from my job would see me the next week, month or year would ask me, "You still here?" On the surface, I thought I was being mocked or ridiculed, but I later realized their question was really one of hope. Underlying each query was the hope that just maybe, it was possible to achieve your dreams. Maybe it was more believable if someone who was in the same boat made it. I remember one colleague admitted a lot of people told him they were going to start their own business and soon retire, only to still work in the same building five years later. Now that I think of it, I believe that talk motivated me to work even harder to find my way out, realizing someone did not believe I could do it. In the end, I now know that his opinion of what was or wasn't possible had absolutely nothing to do with what I believed was possible for me. That's how you must believe, as well.

Jackie and I once took our son, Jordan, and niece, Danielle, to Kings Dominion Amusement Park in Virginia. Danielle, a few years older than Jordan, accompanied him on the Anaconda roller-coaster. Jordan was young and had never ridden a roller-coaster of this magnitude. Jackie and I anxiously watched and waited outside near the exit. Twenty-minutes later, they came out. We were relieved. Then we watched as they went right back around to the entrance and rode again. Then, they exited and went back to the entrance and rode again. They rode again for a total of four times! Jordan had replaced his fear with action!

We all have more power and control than we realize. Every farmer knows the principles of "sowing and reaping" are vital for success in the fields. Seed planting must be done with deliberate planning and limited time available in the fall. Most of us tend to be reactive than proactive, and the results can even be fatal if we're not careful. Take the initiative to get what you want out of life simply by taking a proactive stance on what is important to you and do it!

Once we have taken the bold step to take deliberate action after what we want, we must be willing to keep doing it until the evidence starts to appear. One thing I believe causes people to fail it is a lack of persistence. It is easy to start an endeavor, invest valuable resources such as time and money, and then get discouraged when results of your efforts do not initially materialize. Why should we keep going when there is no visible evidence that it's working? Persistence is connected to decisions of the heart. Thus, we tend to trust more of what we envision through our hearts, than what we see through our eyes. Vision and sight are not the same. The bible speaks to the power of vision. Man without *vision* shall perish, not man without *sight*.

Sight can be deceiving. Russell Cromwell's *Acres of Diamonds* tells the story of the farmer who, after being frustrated with too many rocks on his potato farm, set out looking for riches in faraway lands, never realizing that what he desired was already in abundance on his existing farm. What he thought were rocks were actually diamonds! Similarly, the story of the Chinese Bamboo Tree describes the daily watering of a plant that showed no evidence of growth. The owner was mocked and ridiculed for consistently watering the plant day in and day out for 5 years. However, in the 5th year, the plant grew 90-feet. What sight could not see was the growth that was taking place in the plant root system below the ground to prepare it for its meteoric rise. So, seeing is not always believing. Therefore, when it comes to persistent action, you must be willing to trust what you do not see. Whether your goal is to lose weight, become a bodybuilder, run a 26-mile marathon, or start a business, you must be willing to stay the course and follow what John Maxwell describes as your established "daily agenda" to the goal. Keep going and whatever you do, trust your grind!

Dreams Never Die

While on the path to your desired goals and dreams, we also need to be able to forget certain things along the way. It is interesting that we tend to remember negative or unwanted events. The subconscious mind essentially goes into avoidance or fight mode towards perceived negative situations and events that may have caused us physical or emotional trauma in the past to keep it from happening again. As the saying goes, "a cat, once it sits on a hot stove, will not sit on a cold one either." For example, one major personal baggage obstacle has never been more apparent than in failed relationships. Potentially healthy relationships may never develop due to the mind's ability to remember failed ones. This includes the business owner who refuses partnerships due to failed past partnerships. This way of thinking might obstruct the benefits of fresh opportunities. Be willing to release the negative past (not forget) to embrace new opportunities with an open mind. Just as a flight on a plane with limited storage that can only allow one carryon bag, if you show up at the airport with eight, you would be forced to check seven of them. Check your unwanted negative past experiences, reserving the positive ones for your journey.

Additionally, it is rare for long-term success to be achieved on the first try. While expecting to win is always the goal, those who succeed are willing to endure whatever number of attempts necessary to get what they want. You must be willing to forget previous failed attempts along the way to the goal. Major league baseball is a great example of instituting the element of temporary amnesia for success. A batter who averages a 300-score batting average (30 percent) or higher is considered a superstar, earning millions of dollars a year. What is interesting is, a 300 average means he failed 70 percent of the time. Each time a batter steps to the plate, he must forget all previous attempts to focus on the opportunity at hand. He must have temporary amnesia while at the plate. I remember having a basketball shirt that read on the front, "When you're on, shoot!" On the back it read, "When you're off, shoot 'til you get on!" You must overcome the mind's attempts to protect you from thinking of failed attempts when pursuing your dreams. At the same time, you need to be able to filter in the positive lessons that can be applied to our next attempt.

Talk to any track star and they will agree that to look back during a race can cause you to lose the race. Far too often we spend valuable time reviewing our past failures instead of focusing on the goal or destination in front of us. When you focus, it creates momentum that can cause even more acceleration and drive towards your destination. Remember Newton's first law, "an object will stay in motion or remain at rest unless acted upon by some external source." If we stay focused in going forward, you will continue to go forward. If you are looking back, the opposite is also true. The Apostle Paul in the Bible states, "… forgetting those things that are behind, I press to the mark." Make the quality commitment to run your race without looking back. You won't need a rearview mirror. What's behind you is not important.

CHAPTER SEVEN
Failing Forward

What's your attitude when you fail? Does it excite you or are you discouraged? Growing up, for a long time, my attitude towards failure was one of disappointment. It was personal. I hated to lose in anything I did back then, and I still hate to lose today. However, I now have a much better understanding of winning and losing. There are some lessons in life that can only be learned by failing. The book, *Go for No*, talks about how most people look to avoid failure thinking that by avoiding it they are getting closer to success. It is not true at all. To succeed, you must go through temporary failure to arrive at success. To avoid or put distance between you and failing does not bring you closer to your goals, failing does. Once I was willing to embrace that failing was not a bad thing, but a necessary rite of passage, I moved forward with decisiveness and conviction once presented with the Tropical Smoothie Café opportunity. I gave myself permission to fail, if necessary, with the realization that my dream to be in business for myself was worth whatever price there would be. I was willing to increase my failure rate knowing I would get to my goal sooner. Instead of hoping to minimize failures, maximize them. Only keep in mind a "break glass" strategy for emergencies. There may be times when you'll have to abort a certain approach along the way and by breaking the glass, you'll open your mind to more creative methods to reach your unchanged destination. Most people would agree they are here to do something special; however, it appears what they struggle with most are the actual orders they have been given. Sometimes you will fail, but you should always remember that failing does not make you a failure. You show me someone with a high failure rate, and I will show you someone headed for greatness! So, keep failing and keep coming up short. Remember that you are here on purpose, and right on course to complete your mission.

Talk to any basketball player and you will find that pick-up games were their proving grounds. Local basketball courts are known for attracting star talent and you must be on your best game to get out there. It's where legends are made. Sometimes, there were opportunities to play one-on-one with another player, and these games could be just as intense as an actual game, depending on the player. One thing's for sure, whether you were playing a full team game or just isolated one-on-one, to compete you had to be willing to run-it-back or give yourself a second chance. The opportunity to get a second chance to compete if you lost was an opportunity to improve in areas that may have cost you the first game. When it comes to your dreams, you must look for opportunities to run-it-back. Run-it-back after a failed job interview attempt. Run-it-back after a failed relationship or college test scores. No matter how impossible the odds, if there's time on the clock, you have an opportunity to run it back.

Be willing to do things better than before. Steady and continuous improvement most times ends with positive results. Evaluate your means and methods and be honest with what you find. If you did not put in the time to get a 100 percent on the exam, then maybe consider dedicating more time to studying. If an exercise or goal was missed, recommit, and get back on track. Two lumberjacks in a race to see who could cut down the most trees started out evenly, but the winner cut down almost twice the number as the loser. When asked why such a dominant performance, the winner stated that he was initially behind but took the time to sharpen his axe, while his opponent did not. Be willing to sharpen your axe along the journey. You must also be willing to minimize those factors that can weaken your ability to succeed. Oftentimes, distractors like television, entertainment events, and certain leisure activities can be a detriment to your goals. You may have to miss a birthday party or two or send a card for the next celebration instead of attending in person. Cell phones and social media platforms are also areas that can adversely impact our goals. By minimizing some of these unintentional distractors, you will become laser-focused on the tasks in front of you and gain momentum towards accomplishing the goal at hand.

With so many negative events happening around us each day, it's no wonder that we tend to think of things from a negative perspective instead of a positive one. Thoughts such as, "What if doesn't work?" "What if I'm wrong?" "Suppose I'm not accepted to the School?" "What if I invest my savings and it doesn't work?" These and countless others go through our minds each day when there's also an equally positive thought that exists. Are you ready for your success? Every farmer knows to expect the positive more than the negative. They must have harvesting machinery already in place before the harvest arrives. Tractors, trucks, processing equipment and delivery must be planned well before the first leaf comes out of the ground. Now is the perfect time to plan for your future success. Go ahead and purchase the outfit you plan to wear after losing the weight. Get the brochures and restaurant menus for that hotel and restaurant in Hawaii you've dreamed of your whole life. Whatever it is you'd like to have, expect it and get started on receiving it right now.

Ever wonder why we are afraid to take chances and pursue what we really want? Most of us treat failing as if it should be embarrassing to admit and avoided at all costs. All through school we're conditioned to not fail, or that to do so was not a good thing. Those who achieved A's in class were rewarded while those who got F's were not. So, it stands to reason that as adults we still make it a point to avoid failing as much as possible to ensure we're accepted and are in "good standing" with society. However, I'm not so sure that avoiding failure has turned out to be a good thing. Just the opposite. By intentionally making decisions that will minimize the possibility of failing, we also find ourselves setting goals that are attainable, a good thing, however such goal setting does not allow us to stretch into something we're capable of becoming. To become someone you've never been, you must be willing to do something you've never done. In doing so, failing is required. Failing is how we learn. By avoiding failing, we deprive ourselves of the necessary information needed to succeed. Lacking this information, fear typically fills the void known as the "unknown," and we avoid fear when it appears. So, our attitude towards failing tends to make it something that should be avoided as much as possible and, as a result, our goals as well.

By facing our fear of failure, we put ourselves on the path towards finding what we need to move forward. By embracing multiple failures, we demonstrate our faith and willingness to grow towards something new. Repeat failures can generate positive energy once we evaluate them in the proper context of growth. Embrace repeat failures. Don't get discouraged nor lose faith when things don't turn out as you had hoped. Each shortfall produces the opportunity for even greater success if you look for the signs. Remember, failing does not make you a failure. Whether it be a weight loss goal, new business venture, novel or desire to succeed in politics, be willing to do your part. Fail as often as necessary to get what you want. The power of repetition aligns perfectly with perseverance when we're focused on the *why* of our actions. Get started, stay steady and don't quit no matter what. With continued repetition, you'll soon be able to accelerate your efforts due to increased proficiencies, a powerful by-product of doing an action repeatedly. Potential weaknesses can also be identified sooner and corrected more promptly.

It's not always easy to recognize or accept the fact that your first few attempts at a goal may not work at all. Discussing less than favorable results with others is difficult. No one wants to admit they did not reach their stated goal. Yet there is a liberating feeling when you can honestly say you missed the mark. Your attitude will make all the difference. Sharing the speed bumps along the journey not only inspires others, but constantly reminds you of your personal commitment and willingness to overcome to become. If you share unwanted results with a flair for overcoming barriers to success, you'll find enormous confidence and power available for future attempts.

Maintaining a positive attitude is sometimes all you need to go to the next level of your journey. This thought process is even more impactful for the person who's made the decision to win. Despite the visible results, consistently going after what you want increases belief and admiration in observers. No entity is better known for their demonstration of action than the world's greatest Army, the U.S. Army's 82nd Airborne Infantry. If you could ever speak with a member of this prestigious group, you'll immediately notice they live and breathe action. It's in their DNA. With an incredible can-do attitude for mission accomplishment, they jump into the night air without focusing on their own well-being, but the overall goal of the team. Each understands how the individual actions of one can have an enormous impact on the team. Talk to a Jump Master such as my dear friend, Mike Gold, and they'll tell you not only is leadership by example required, it's expected.

CHAPTER EIGHT
Ridicule vs. Reward

Ridicule is required. When it comes to having a big dream, it will always be attached to the ridicule of others who do not understand what you see. The price tag for dreaming big can be an expensive one, mainly because the bigger the dream, the bigger the disbelief found in others. I once attended a cookout and overheard one guest sharing with another that I always talk about going into business, but they had not seen where I was actually running one. Ridicule in this context is not so much directly communicated to you (unless it's a family member), but more through indirect conversations through others. If not careful, you could start thinking everyone's having these same kinds of conversations about you. However, such conversations rarely occur, But, unchecked, the thought can grow out of control, commanding more attention than it should. Do not get discouraged. This means you are heading in the right direction.

We tend to be fine with our dreams and goals as long as we don't encounter others who either don't share our vision or support what we're looking to achieve (aka "haters") as in the example above. The adverse impact of embracing negative thoughts in our midst can be of major consequence, causing lost time, momentum, and quitting altogether. This negative energy can become so destructive that pursuing our goal seems impossible or a waste of time.

Picture a rose garden full of beautiful roses. To preserve it, it must be protected with fertilizer, pruning and watering. When it's not maintained, weeds appear out of nowhere. With no fertilizer, seeds, or watering, they just show up. Unchecked, the weeds eventually choke out the roses. So, it is with our dreams and goals, we must perform daily maintenance on them by associating with positive and supporting acquaintances while distancing ourselves from unsupportive haters. Be willing to perform regular maintenance on your goals. If unchecked, like weeds, negative becomes automatic.

Where does this desire come from? You were "designed for accomplishment and endowed with seeds of greatness!" – Zig Ziglar. Like the corn seed that has no specific direction nor guidance knows to grow once planted, so it is with you. Your very design was intended for doing something great, and the more you do, the more you'll do. Og Mandino, in "The Greatest Miracle in the World", states in his "God Memorandum" you are a miracle, and your uniqueness should be embraced and celebrated. Like the Mona Lisa, you are an original, so embrace your rarity!

In most cases our dreams involve sharing them with others we care about, namely friends, neighbors and relatives or FN&Rs. Whether it be a beautiful new home, a boat, or vacation, we envision sharing our success with others we love and admire. No one merely thinks of having a 20-foot dining table with a placement for one. FN&Rs can have significant influence however on our belief system if we're not careful. We value their opinions greatly, and if we don't receive their endorsement nor approval, it can affect our own decision-making. When FN&Rs don't understand, nor believe in our goals and dreams, we must be strong and focused enough to proceed despite their lack of understanding. Unchecked their influence can keep you in an average mindset, comfortable with the status quo. Be sure to have a strong inoculation plan against negative FN&Rs. Remember, most negative thinking people don't even know they think negative. The adage "familiarity breeds contempt" is so true. You have a goal or dream that you've been working on for a while, but you have no results or evidence of success. For those who think they know you, it is difficult for them to see you in any other way than what they remember from the past. FN&Rs, in particular, will have a hard time embracing your new-found enthusiasm and drive for success. Most will not want to accept the changes in you mainly because to do so means their world has also changed. Birthday parties, family gatherings and celebrations normally attended may fall by the wayside for anyone chasing the dream, and these changes are not easily accepted by those in your inner circle. Don't get discouraged if they do not accept nor believe the changes in you. Remain confident in the "new you" and eventually, they too will eventually comply. Allow them to have their space until they're ready. You may have to start out with others outside of your inner circle to move forward without prejudice. If so, embrace the fact that you cannot lose a friend by gaining new ones. No candle is ever diminished when it lights another.

On your success journey, you are also going to encounter the three C's: criticize, condemn and complain. These three can be very damaging if not addressed early. What's interesting about them is they can appear at any time and without prior notice. People will criticize change they don't believe is possible, condemn those who have the courage to stand their ground in the pursuit, and complain aloud when they see the change happening. The three C's are most damaging when originated by your FN&Rs, those closest to you. Recognizing they exist is the first defense against them, followed by putting distance between you and the originators. It's much harder to convince those who've known you to change to a new way of thinking. John 4:44 states, "A prophet is without honor in his own country." You may have to leave the familiar to make your mark. Know that by doing so, you'll create a greater opportunity to return. Don't be offended by their lack of belief but understand they may not see what you see right now. Use their disbelief as fuel for your success fire!

Your dreams are delicate and require protection from negative thoughts which, like weeds mentioned earlier, could choke the life out of the most beautiful rose. Their impact can be so strong that they continue in our minds long after they were uttered. Be vigilant and on guard for negative opinions and thoughts. Negative opinions of others are just that, opinions. They speak with no true concern whether their thoughts may be damaging. You must be strong and on guard for negative opinions, keeping unsupportive thoughts to your dreams to a minimum. Remember, the empty wagon makes the most noise.

It doesn't really matter if people don't believe you when you tell them what you plan to do, if you believe. As we've discussed, the opinions of others are as varied as there are people who have them. Once you're confident and secure with conviction, whether others believe you will not matter. Likewise, if you do believe them and it's contrary to what you want to achieve, ask yourself is that really what you want? For them to be right? Of course, not! If what they believe and say are contrary to what you want, then don't give their negative thoughts life and power to make it come true. Be all in for what you want and others will gravitate to you. Embrace an "all eyes on me" mentality and be excited about your success growth.

Whenever someone laughs at you or attempts to minimize your goals and dreams, use it as fuel and keep moving forward. Action coupled with enthusiasm eliminates fear and activates the three positive C's of success: courage, confidence and commitment. To achieve anything worthwhile, start with the *Mirror Effect*. There's nothing more impactful to achieving success than the power of how you see yourself. Whoever's looking back at you will determine what you achieve. Is it someone confident, empowered by the three positive C's of success? How does the reflection speak to you? Bold? Unshaken? To get what you want, make sure you're in perfect lockstep with the one committed to win in everything you've ever achieved. The Winner in you knows how and all you need to do is make sure you connect with them daily. Accepting personal responsibility is the beginning and is always a choice. Everything you've achieved up until now has been accomplished that way, and everything you will achieve will, likewise, be because you did.

If someone offers you unsolicited advice, then you are speaking with a hater. Unsolicited advice, no matter how gentle the delivery, is still criticism. Advice only has value for the person seeking it. No need to be confrontational nor defensive when engaging them. Politely distance yourself or do your best to refrain from discussing your dreams around negative-thinking people. Once you take authority for your dreams, you can confidently face your haters. In the end, they will believe what you believe.

Taking a stance to be first may also lend itself to the 2R's – resistance and ridicule. The more unbelievable the dream, the stronger the 2R's! However, the more unbelievable the goal, the bigger and sweeter the victory. Observe the masses, then do the opposite! No matter how much study and education an army paratrooper may have, there's only one way to really know the security of his or her parachute. They've got to jump!

Be willing to do exactly whatever causes you to pause. If you're opening a new business, get the plans together so you can find the capital you need to get the doors open. If you want to travel the world, get the brochures, contact the hotels and let them know you're on the way. That new car or new home has your name on it and is waiting on you! Once started, you won't be able to stop. Momentum will keep moving you to the next opportunity. The true power is in the doing because the more you do, the more you will do! We demonstrate our faith by doing, and you have the power.

One of my goals at our café was to serve 1 million customers in our first 4 years of operation, and I set out immediately to tell everyone of the goal. A customer asked, "Exactly how do you plan to accomplish the 1 million served sales mark?" My answer: "I have no idea. I must find the people who can help me figure out the details on how to do it." You do not need to have all the answers of how the goal will be accomplished. That will come at the appointed time. What is important to realize is you must be willing to set the goal and know your why.

The responses we received from customers were incredible. Some customers volunteered to contribute to our goal by sharing the goal via their social media platforms. Others told friends, neighbors and relatives to patron our café since we had an established goal that included community involvement. The momentum has continued to grow, and we passed the mark in May. Now the goal is 5 Million! It is a natural tendency to want to be part of something significant and worthwhile and by sharing with others, you will unleash an incredible level of people power to help you reach your goals. Once you set yourself on fire, everyone will come help you burn! Win over your number one customer. The one who's there day in and day out. The one who you speak to all day every day. The only one you must convince to your way of thinking – you! In getting to where you want to be, you must realize and accept the fact that you're the one that's going to make it happen. It's a personal decision that only you can make. When evaluating your abilities, be sure to give yourself extra credit for making quality decisions. Remember all your previous successes and recall the same energy of conviction you tapped into to accomplish whatever you have achieved up to now. Look yourself in the mirror and say, "I'm that one!"

"The Guy in the Glass"
When you get what you want in your struggle for self,
And the world makes you King for a day,
Then go to the mirror and look at yourself,
And see what that guy has to say.

Clement T. Troutman

For it isn't your Father, or Mother, or Wife,
Who judgement upon you must pass.
The feller whose verdict counts most in your life
Is the guy staring back from the glass.

He's the feller to please, never mind all the rest,
For he's with you clear up to the end,
And you've passed your most dangerous, difficult test
If the guy in the glass is your friend.

You may be like Jack Horner and "chisel" a plum,
And think you're a wonderful guy,
But the man in the glass says you're only a bum
If you can't look him straight in the eye.

You can fool the whole world down
the pathway of years,
And get pats on the back as you pass,
But your final reward will be heartaches and tears
If you've cheated the guy in the glass.
Dale Wimbrow (c) 1934
1895-1954

CHAPTER NINE
Change is Inevitable

"Once you change the way you look at things, the things you look at change!"

When you decide to go after your dream, there must be a willingness to change. That powerful computer between your ears we spoke of earlier is designed to sabotage your efforts at every turn when it comes to change. Our minds are conditioned to treat the familiar as the safe zone, while the unfamiliar as the fear zone. Since dreams are initially unfamiliar to our minds, we subconsciously label these emotions as fear, when it really represents the mind's response to a new or unknown behavior. Once these new thoughts or ideas become familiar to our minds through the process of repetition, they then get recategorized as safe.

A major challenge for most of us is accepting the need to change. Remember, the mind embraces the familiar, so to truly change requires deliberate and consistent effort long after the desire to do a thing has passed. What if it doesn't work the first, second, third or fourth time? What are you willing to change to make it work? Would you change your career, skill set, appearance, associations, or the vehicle that will take you where you'd like to go? You may have to change some or all to get you to where you want to be. You don't necessarily have to forgo lifelong friendships and family, but you should evaluate whether such associations support your dreams or detract from them. Successful people make a commitment to align themselves with right people who support and enhance their goals, rather than those that might minimize them. A good litmus test to determine whether you're in the right company or not is whether those in your inner circle encourage you to speak freely of your goals or, contrarily, you feel compelled to remain silent around them when you really want to speak in fear that such talk will not be well-received. Still, there was always at least one person there who wanted to talk business.

Change is inevitable. You may have to even change the type of business you once decided was your chosen vehicle for success, as did Conrad Hilton. A great book on the process of change (or lack thereof) I read was, *Who Moved My Cheese*. The book's key characters are "Sniff and Scurry" and "Hem and Haw". Sniff and Scurry quickly embrace change, whereas; Hem and Haw were reluctant to do so. In the end, a change of direction does not mean giving up on the dream, but to recognize when a given course might lead to a dead end. Anyone traveling by train must decide once notified the bridge is out ahead whether to get off the train or not. Even if you do nothing, you've still made a decision. Decide. Be willing to be flexible in your pursuits. For, one day your purpose will collide with your destiny and you must be prepared to be different from the person you are right now. This is not a bad thing. Most times we think in terms of not wanting to change once we're successful. The reality is you have no choice. You will not be the same person you were before reaching your goals. The person you are becoming can reach their dreams. The person you are right now, maybe not. Otherwise, you would have done it already.

The good news is there's nothing wrong with change. It's inevitable, and with regards to your dreams, required. Just be willing to do so, removing unwanted behaviors that block your dreams, and replacing them with positive new behaviors that yield success. Success will not change you, but you must change to be successful. So, go ahead and change your mind! Change will also take place in others and how they interact to you. Why? Because you've changed. Be receptive to the realization that others who perceive you differently, because you will be different. Now is the time to consider how good or how big your success can be. How big can it be? Is there a maximum level? How many people will potentially be impacted by what you want to do? It takes guts to do something big that's never been done, and that's exactly what you must have. Go get what you believe, not what others believe for you. The best way to believe is by acting. Your belief will grow the more you do whatever it is you may be afraid of. If public speaking is something that frightens you, then start talking. The brain learns only one way that I know of, and that is through repetition. Start living the way you want to live, and you will live that way. While planning is an important element in the success process, many people have devised incredible plans and designs that never got off the paper. But a doer is more focused on the results of the action than the planning. There will be times when you won't be able to plan until after you've taken action of some sort to gain the necessary knowledge. Remember, a rocket travels off its course over 90 percent of its flight, but it has a gyroscope to assist it on the journey, correcting its course each time it ventures off the flight route. Be sure not to spend too much time in the planning phase. Once you've got a decision in place, get your aircraft out on the runway and prepare for takeoff!

CHAPTER TEN
Success: A Common Language

While we may have some attributes that are similar in nature, we are uniquely designed. Like snowflakes, no two people are the same. Your rarity is a gift from God. Yet, far too often, we think we know others, especially those in our inner circles such as friends, neighbors, and relatives. However, the complexities of genetic design make each encounter with a new person a unique experience. Imagine if every computer or smart phone on earth had its own software different from every other computer. It would be very difficult to communicate with one another. You would not be able to serve your customers and, therefore, would have no chance of doing business. People who win speak a common success language and are attracted to those who also like to win. Decide to win, and you will attract to you the type of people necessary to win. Understand and embrace the qualities winners have in common ...

First, winners are emotionally stable. Continuous development of your mind to its full potential, unlocks unlimited capacity and creativity. In today's world, it's amazing what we have been able to accomplish due to emerging technologies in computers. From advances in health care with robotics, to banking with smart phones, it's difficult to do almost anything without technology. Computers and the power of the internet have created a whole new world of possibilities. Yet, despite these remarkable advances, the most powerful computing source on earth has been in our possession our entire lives and lying between our two ears. Our brains have unlimited capacity, and the subconscious mind represents a vast and uncharted territory still waiting to be explored.

Secondly, winners enhance their physical well-being. When it comes to success, our physical well-being plays a pivotal role in our journey. Proper rest, diet and exercise all ensure that we are ready for maximum performance and durability when required. The importance of healthy lungs adds to the quality of the oxygen we inhale, stimulating creative thoughts in the brain. When we feel good about ourselves, we think positive thoughts. On the contrary, when we don't feel good about ourselves, we think about negative, non-productive thoughts. So, feeling good physically will stimulate good thoughts and creativity.

Next, winners develop and increase financial resources. It's interesting that when speaking with people, I am amazed at how many do not plan to win financially. They place limited importance on having money but want the personal freedoms, security, time with family, recreation, philanthropy, that having it can bring. The ability to have these are all greatly impacted by our financial positions in life whether we want to believe it or not. We spend our most valuable resource, time, looking to acquire it. Having a financial growth plan is not only a good idea but is necessary to further your dreams and goals. There are countless under-privileged communities or worthy causes in the world, and all require money. Increasing our respect for it, we can then learn how to retain and grow it. How much is up to you, but remember, even if all your goals are met financially, someone else can use whatever you have left over. I remember a speech I heard from motivational speaker Les Brown. Someone commented that money wasn't everything and his response was: "No, but it's right up there with oxygen." Money is a tool that, when used properly, can do a lot of good. You can't feed the hungry from an empty plate.

Finally, winners attach an achievement date to their goals. We must be willing to assign specific times to our dreams and goals to move them into the planning and execution phases. Would you take a vacation trip without an estimated time of arrival? Most people wouldn't and, likewise, your dreams must have an established completion date no matter how intimidating it may be. Once determined, we immediately start working towards it. The good news is, if we fail to accomplish the goal in the stated timeframe, we have permission to reset the estimated time again and, if necessary, again until we reach it. What is your completion date?

CHAPTER ELEVEN
Perseverance: A Made-up Mind

"...but this one thing I do, forgetting those things which are behind, and reaching forth unto those things which are before..., I press toward the mark ..." ~ *Philippians 3:13-14*

"Insanity is doing the same thing over and over and expecting a different result." – Albert Einstein. However, I'm not so sure that this definition is totally true. There are times when doing things over and over, in a consistent and persistent manner, can yield amazing results that totally contradict this definition. Faith is demonstrated through the process of repetition. Take the story of the Chinese Bamboo Tree, for example.

Clement T. Troutman

There was a farmer who bought a small Chinese bamboo tree with instructions that simply read, "For maximum growth, water daily." The farmer followed the instructions to the letter, consistently watering the tree every day for 5 years. However, it took five years to see evidence of its growth. The tree grew 90-feet in a span of just 60-days, but the farmer had to be committed to the diligent watering instructions for 5-years to witness the exponential grow in year five. He watered the tree on faith.

Another misconception is that attempting an action repeatedly implies failure when it can also imply unshaken belief that the goal is possible. Action backed by persistence is virtually unstoppable.

"Nothing in this world can take the place of persistence. Talent will not: nothing is more common than unsuccessful men with talent. Genius will not; unrewarded genius is almost a proverb. Education will not: the world is full of educated derelicts. Persistence and determination alone are omnipotent." ~ *Calvin Coolidge*

Dreams Never Die

Growing up, my son Jordan wanted to play the piano. Since neither Jackie nor I played, he took piano lessons. While observing him during his recitals, we were always amazed how well he played. How was it that he could play so well although his parents were musically challenged? He played a lot! That's the only way to learn the piano. Whether it's mastering the piano or being number one in your class, if you're willing to be committed to the practice, you will find yourself becoming a master of your dreams. Expect and embrace the mistakes along the way.

It will always take more effort in the beginning of your journey. How much effort depends on how bad you want it. What I believe keeps people from starting is not that it takes work, but if the goal is lofty, they focus on the magnitude of the goal instead of just starting the process. You will achieve more of the things you desire by being dedicated to the daily small things than the big ones. Whether big or small goals, you must be willing to start the process. Maybe the goal is to run a 10-kilometer marathon one day, but you've never been a distance runner. You might want to start by running to the corner of your block first. Over time, you'd be able to run 10 blocks, then 10 kilometers. One thing's for sure, if you never take the action to run to the end of your block, the marathon will most likely never come to fruition. So, be committed to the start, not concerned about the finish line. Just get out there and go! Accelerate your efforts without focusing on mistakes. You will improve as you go and create more energy and power to continue by using your "Mighty Mo"– momentum!

When in the action zone, you cannot make any provisions for failure in your thought process. The fall football season is a perfect example of being in the "action zone." Teams line up on 4th down with 1-yard to go on the 1-yard line, and both teams have an expectation. One to score a touchdown, the other to stop them from scoring. Which team succeeds is not as important as the thought process they must both embrace, not to fail in the attempt. Both teams tap into energy reserves they didn't know they had. Each will be motivated by either an overwhelming desire to win or an equally powerful fear of losing. You will likewise tap into these emotions while operating in your action zone. When you take deliberate action towards your dreams and goals others are likewise inspired to act. People admire those who go after their dreams, even if they themselves may not have the confidence to go after their own. The fact that you were willing to take a stand for what you want and pay the full price for it creates a positive legacy, even if you fail. Hence, others are freed to take risks and go after their dreams by witnessing your decision to act on yours.

Once you start, don't stop. Keep going. It takes much less effort to keep going after you start than to restart. Then, once a quality decision is made and you've started, it will be necessary to have reminders of why you made your decision. Whether it was to create better financial opportunities for your family, impact your community in a positive way, create a legacy or just live life on your own terms, you'll eventually hit what is referred to as "the wall." Talk to anyone in the track & field world that has ever run the 400-meter dash and they will tell you that there's a point in the race – the back stretch – where runners hit what's called, the wall. This is the place in the race where it is difficult to maintain momentum while facing a head wind, and runners tend to hit the greatest amount of resistance during the run. At this point, runners have trained for this difficult part of the race through strength training. You will have similar experiences while on your journey, so be sure to prepare mentally (and physically) for your trip. Make sure not to embrace thoughts of stopping or quitting during these temporary resistance periods. Things may slow down a bit and although you've given maximum effort, results are fewer than during the start phase. The excitement about your decision leaves and you're left with the actual grind phase. To sustain your drive, rely on discipline to keep moving forward. Even when you're not seeing progress, you must stay committed to your grind. If a restart becomes necessary, so be it. Realize your decision to reach your dreams was a final one and no one can stop you, but you.

Keeping a focused perspective on where you're headed is very important to reaching your goals. Far too often we tend to look back to what's familiar to obtain validation for breaking new ground or charting new paths. While this is probably a natural thought, it's important to consider the potential of losing focus on the goal each time you do. Suppose a family is driving from New York to Orlando, Florida on vacation and heading South on I-95 through the state of Maryland. Although they have traveled a considerable distance from New York, they still have quite a distance to go to reach their destination. To reach their goal, they must remain focused on the road ahead, with limited thought of what they've left behind. Not to mention, it can be very costly and even dangerous to spend too much time looking in the rearview mirror. Be willing to imagine living in your future and how it's going to be so much more than how you're living right now. The more you can focus on the goal, the closer it will become. So, stay focused on what's ahead.

Likewise, once you accomplish your goal, share it with others. While most people shy away from doing so to avoid the agitation of being considered boastful or self-serving, you must do it. People believe what they see, and even if they don't speak it aloud they are inwardly saying, "Show me it's possible." Showing evidence of your success is not an arrogant act, but one of proof and integrity; and you should be generous in the displaying of your success with all humility. Doing so will instantly give others hope.

In April 2016, I stated we would operate a million-dollar café. Without even a location, I also proclaimed we would be a top-producing café in the franchise chain. Not to mention we had no background in neither traditional franchising nor the restaurant industry. Anyone willing to listen probably chalked it up to me being a naive and unknowing new franchisee – a freshman who couldn't possibly know how unlikely such a goal might be.

As mentioned earlier, everything changed after we officially opened our doors, and we've consistently been the highest-producing café in the franchise's 20-plus year history. Some may consider it luck, but now that the evidence is visible, I assume people now also believe.

Ever thought about the meaning of going the distance? I think most of us think about it in a general sense, but most times we really don't consider the long-term aspects of our decision-making. For instance, when I made the decision to eat a hamburger and fries, something that used to be an irresistible passion of mine, never once did I consider the long-term implications of that decision. How much red meat would I be eating over the course of my life or how much fat content ingested over a lifetime of fries was never a consideration. Yet, most of us have made many seemingly short-term decisions with long-term consequences. Imagine if the decision was a long-term decision to drink eight glasses of water a day or eat an apple a day for 40-years? How much better could our health possibly be? The same holds true when it comes to financial success. The person who commits to saving just one hour of income each day will one day be a millionaire, and no one can stop them!

One factor that may adversely impact our ability to persevere is placing limits on the number of attempts we're willing to make to get a desired outcome. Whether making the decision consciously or subconsciously, many times we limit our own success by only being willing to try a certain number of times. This usually comes from logic based on equating our attempts with stored historical data in our minds. What if you didn't know how many attempts were considered enough? What if there was no historical basis for attempts for you to compare your actions? Would you stop trying if it's something you really wanted to do? Would you care how many attempts were necessary to reach your goal? No. The number of times would not matter. As long as you have the capacity, keep attempting until you get what you want. To persevere, when you fail you are going to have to go again and again until you succeed.

Most people do not respond very well to the doubts and criticisms others may express about their goals and the lack of ability they have in reaching them. I don't respond well to them either. It's amazing how some people, usually those in your inner circle of whom you trust, and respect are the same ones that utter their disapproval of your dreams. In almost every such case, they offer their unsolicited opinions and advice under the guise of caring for you. Once we accept the fact that unsolicited advice is considered criticism, we can then start to take emotional control over these "hater comments." Make the quality decision to believe in you more than believing in them.

A small, two-letter word with immense power, the word *so,* can help override unwanted negative opinions instantly. For example, say you're looking to start a business and you may not have the necessary startup capital to make it a reality, a dear well-meaning friend comments, "You don't have enough money to start a business." You may take control of the conversation immediately by simply replying, "So!" Let's just say you didn't score high enough on your college exam to get into the college you wanted, and others say, "Your grades are not high enough." The only response necessary is the word, "So." If they warn you it may not work ... "So." You may lose your money." ... "So." "They may quit on you." ... "So!" "You don't have experience." ... "So!" Unleash the power of *so* and free yourself from the doubts of others so that you can focus on your destination without reservation.

If you look up the word stubborn, you'll find many definitions. One I found reads, "... having or showing a dogged determination not to change one's attitude or position on something, especially despite good arguments or reasons to do so." Other terms used are *hard-headed*, *set in your ways*, *pig-headed*, etc. I have been called all of them. Most times we associate stubbornness with a negative unwanted attitude, but does it have to be negative? What if someone's stubborn enough to stay the course towards their dreams or find a cure to a disease? When it comes to being successful, you're going to have to be stubborn enough to overcome distractions and obstacles, both physical and mental. How it's looked upon by others usually depends on the timing. In the beginning, expect to be labeled stubborn because there may not be any visible proof of what you're working towards. For example, the business idea you have has been turned down repeatedly at every business proposal you've done over the last 10 years. Most would wonder why you continue to try when no one seems interested. In this context, one would most likely label you as stubborn or set in your ways. But what if the 11th year resulted in the opportunity of a lifetime, such as a major contract with the government or a Fortune 500 company, emerged with a desperate demand for your product or service? History would probably point to you as being visionary, committed, unyielding, or uncompromising in your belief, all implying positive and admirable qualities. What's the difference between the two scenarios? The results. When it comes to your freedom, you must be stubborn enough today to be admired as a visionary tomorrow.

With perseverance also comes will power that speaks whether outwardly or internally, "I will not be denied." Will power from the heart generates an emotional decision and passion to go into action that can't be stopped. The price is not important when it's a matter of will. The decision has been made and the job must be completed. Having a competitive spirit also influences will power. Those who naturally compete in athletics or academics are familiar with this emotional level and know how to tap into it when needed. The student that achieved a 99 percent score on the test when the goal was 100 percent, taps into the "I will not be denied" power phase on the next test. I remember watching NBA Basketball Champion, Kobe Bryant miss shots in a playoff game and right after the game, it was reported that he returned to the court and began practicing the shots he missed. The rest of the team had already left the stadium for the night. He had tapped into his "I will not be denied" power. The good news is you don't have to be an academic scholar or NBA champion to access your "I will not be denied" power. It lies waiting in every heart, waiting to go to work for whoever's willing to call on it. It's waiting on you!

Dreams Never Die

Failing or losing can serve as our greatest motivation if properly received and processed. I remember being the fastest kid in our 5th-grade class and competing in the 50-yard dash during student athletics week. Everyone expected me to win. However, when the gun sounded I slipped and came in second place. I almost won, but the other kid beat me to the finish line by a hair. That day, the other kid was awarded the 1st Place Blue Ribbon he had rightfully won, and I received the 2nd Place Red Ribbon. Why is this story important? Many years have passed since that race and I still remember it today as if it were yesterday. While in life we cannot roll back the clock to replay the past, there remains an opportunity to win, despite past failures. The race for success can be run over and over and over until you win. So, if when you find yourself on the losing end of a goal, look in the mirror and go again. Persevere in any endeavor requires steady and consistent activity. The body builder preparing for a competition may take a day or two of rest to rejuvenate fatigued muscles, but will soon return to training. One of many serendipities of being the highest producing café is having crewmembers who are steady, very capable and experienced in their respective positions to help produce consistently high daily volumes. Being steady does not imply that mistakes won't occur. They will occur, but will also create the opportunity to learn, become better, and more efficient. There isn't one member of our team that hasn't made a mistake or two while working at the café. As a matter of fact, we welcome mistakes that are necessary to move on to the next learning phase as long as they aren't continually repeated. Being steady and predictable allows for accurate measurements to be established so that objective improvements may also be made. Inconsistent behaviors should be kept to a minimum while consistency and persistency should be top priorities. Stay steady. By doing so, you'll win every race.

The topic of perseverance could not be discussed without mentioning the story of Bill Porter. Bill Porter was a door-to-door salesman in Portland, Oregon back in the 1950's. Born with cerebral palsy, he was initially unable to gain employment but refused to go on disability. Porter eventually convinced Watkins Incorporated to give him a door-to-door salesman job, selling its products on a seven-mile route in the Portland area. The stories of his relentless determination and drive resulted in him becoming Watkins' top salesman and inspired both books and films of his remarkable story. Shelly Brady's book, *Ten Things I Learned from Bill Porter,* tells the story of how the company's CEO was hosting a convention to motivate its sales force. Bill Porter was there participating in a staged interview, as the CEO believed that if anyone could motivate the sales team base it would be Bill, considering he was earning several times their earning power. The moderator preceded to interview Bill and asked: "Given your handicap, to what do you attribute your remarkable success?" After a lengthy pause to the question, he eventually responded, "What handicap?" Despite his condition, Bill Porter never considered himself handicapped, and he lived his life accordingly with over 40-years of sales with Watkins Incorporated. There's a Bill Porter level of determination in you, too. To persevere towards your goals and dreams, activate your Bill Porter attitude!

I have had the fortune of witnessing, arguably, the greatest basketball player of all time during my lifetime. I watched the greatness of Michael Jordan as he redefined the National Basketball Association. In his book, *I Can't Accept Not Trying*, he expresses his views on fear and describes it only as an illusion. He also goes on to explain that most people think about the consequences more than the opportunity. When focused on the consequences, fear is increased while confidence is eroded. He didn't worry about being embarrassed for missing a big shot or what others would say. He focused on the moment at hand and the opportunity presented. Fear is an emotion that can be conquered by discipline, perseverance, and focus. Michael Jordan practiced with the same intensity he played in games, which is highly unusual for even the most famous athletes. He believed that he would not have performed at the highest level during a game if he had never reached that level during practice. He walked it like he talked it, and that's what I want you to do.

While the world knows the history behind Thomas Edison, less known is the story of his greatest competitor and young apprentice, Nikola Tesla. Tesla was the inventor of alternating current (AC), which became the standard used in homes (Edison was responsible for direct current or DC). After resigning from Edison, Tesla started his own company and was supported by George Westinghouse. Although Tesla was considered the underdog in the electricity war of the 1900s, he gained unprecedented notoriety across the country and revolutionized the electrical industry. Even Edison underestimated his value and potential. Today, the electricity we use is AC – the invention of Tesla, not Edison. The fact that Tesla was more concerned for providing a great product that was safe for the masses was the cornerstone of his success. Embrace being the underdog while in pursuit of your dreams. When you refuse to lose, you automatically activate an emotional power to persevere past unexpected obstacles and barriers. First and foremost is the acknowledgement that to fail and to be a failure are not the same. The act of failing in order to achieve a plan or goal is necessary to succeed, and the reason most people don't succeed is they focus on avoiding failing with the thought that to fail means they have not succeeded. This avoidance is why so few ever reach their intended goals or level of prominence in life. Be willing to embrace failing so you can learn how to succeed. Failure on the other hand, represents giving up or accepting a failing circumstance as a permanent state of being, instead of a temporary setback or learning opportunity. Never succumb to failure. It's not a viable option. Disregard the odds, for they cannot predict the future. To persevere, you must be able to distinguish between failing and failure to succeed.

You must concentrate on your strengths, your most valuable assets. First, identify what is it you do well. Consider the product or service you offer that you know without a doubt has value others will use or would be willing to pay. Maybe you're great at art and you've never shared the passion you have for it with others, or maybe you're a math wizard. Perhaps you're someone who talks a lot and would be a great orator (that would probably be me if you ask anyone who knows me). If writing is something you know without a doubt you can do, that may be your gift to the world. Whatever it is, do it now!

Have you perfected your gift? It took me years to listen when others suggested I write a book. When it comes to your specific gift, you may think that it might not be of great value to others, although it's something you're very passionate about. Why wouldn't others be interested if you are? If it comes to you easily, it may be difficult to place value on it. Your gift does have value, and it's time to share it with the world! Make a commitment today to focus on your gifts and stay in your own unique lane. That is where your greatest strength and opportunities lie.

You have more abilities within you than you think. If you took one seed of corn and placed it in a can and left it on a shelf for 100 years, it would not change. You would find a very old corn seed. But, what if you took that same seed and placed it in soil where it could benefit from the ground's nutrients, water from the rain, and sunlight? It would begin to germinate and grow upward, pushing against impossible odds, through the dirt, until it reaches the surface. It would continue to grow and would eventually sprout a stalk, yielding several ears of corn. Even if it was planted in a field of wheat, the corn seed will stay focused on its mission to grow as corn. How does the corn seed know what to do and when? It knows because it was engineered by God to do what it does, and so were you. You've been given specific orders to do something meaningful that will benefit the world, and only you know what it is. Now is the time to do it.

What if you are right about your new business idea and people do love it? Have you prepared for an onslaught of new business like never before? What if your dream requires you to relocate to another city or state? Are you ready? Statistics report that most new start-up businesses can take a few years before they turn a profit. What if it doesn't take that long? What if your business soars on day one? Are you ready to change? Now is the time to prepare yourself for massive success. It will be waiting for you at the end of your perseverance journey.

"A good man leaveth an inheritance to his children's children: and the wealth of the sinner is laid up for the just." ~ Proverbs 13:22

CHAPTER TWELVE
Success: A Winning Thought Process

If you think of anyone who's ever succeeded at anything, you'll find that, in almost every instance, their success began with a winning thought process. Whether it be in art like Michelangelo, music like Beethoven, theater like Denzel Washington, politics like President Obama, Olympic swimming like Michael Phelps or basketball like Michael Jordan, a winning thought process is the common denominator between all of them. Think about times when you wanted to achieve something badly and achieved it. There was one dominant thought you had, and you adjusted to make it happen. Flexibility and success go hand in hand. You won't find anyone who achieved success that did not have to exhibit a certain degree of flexibility along the way. As the saying goes, "so long as you remain flexible, you'll never get bent out of shape."

Focus on the end goal from the beginning. Expect your road to success to be lined with obstacles. Anytime you set out to do something you've never done, there will most likely be unexpected events that come your way. It would be great if you could know them all in advance but, unfortunately, that's not the way it works. Every owner looks to minimize risk; however, the unknowns may appear at any time. Most times are not convenient at all. For our store, issues with maintaining a steady supply line, storage limitations, staffing shortages and equipment malfunctions, and power outages were just a few of the challenges we faced, and still do. In addition to these normal disconnects common with a new store opening, there were unforeseen challenges stemming from high demand such as, a need for more ice. The recommended standard ice machine we had could not produce ice fast enough to keep up with demand, and we would literally run out of ice – not a good position to be in for a smoothie-producing café. Fortunately, we started our business with built-in contingencies in mind such as, adding two ice heads instead of the traditional one. Still, we had to adjust, borrowing ice from fellow franchisees and neighboring restaurants just to make it to closing. We upgraded our ice machine, again, ultimately replacing the original configuration with a top of the line version capable of producing mass quantities of ice by the hour. We've had refrigerator units and ovens stop working right in the middle of major rush hours while long lines of customers patiently waited in both our lobby and drive-thru. Crew members have called out more often than we ever imagined, causing working staff to miss their scheduled time for breaks, while frustrated customers sought answers. As a leader, you must be durable – yet compassionate – of people who been affected by various events, and you must process each one separately. Contingencies were created and executed for almost every aspect of operations because the model was working incredibly well, not because it wasn't.

Leaders also accept responsibility. In terms of teamwork, the leader assumes leadership. It is not given but taken, and with it comes responsibility for the overall success of the team. It is the leader that sets the tone for a winning culture within the team or group. A leader's influence can be readily seen by looking at those being led. A team cannot achieve beyond the capabilities of its leadership. While certain authorities may be delegated to members of the team, ultimate authority and responsibility always remains with the leader. The gate sentry of a military base stands guard over the entry and exit of all vehicles to and from the base. With his or her delegated authority, the sentry has several options at its disposal for controlling unruly visitors: require the visitor to present identification; detain or arrest the unruly visitor; or even shoot the visitor should deadly force be required. While the sentry has several options for controlling its post, original and final responsibility remains with the General or Commander of the base, who sets overall base policies, including access control to the installation.

We take leadership very seriously in our business, as well. It's important to ensure proper authority is provided with any delegation of power. Managers and Shift Leaders are afforded the necessary levels of authority to do the job of the position; however, we are mindful to monitor and ensure there is no abuse of positional authority or power in the process. Ultimately, the leader must be willing to say, "If it's to be, it's up to me!" Or as I frequently inform our guests, "The crew gets all the credit, while I take all the blame!" As the leader, periodic self-assessments are critical for sustained success and accomplishment, so be sure to keep a mirror nearby. Through it all, Jackie and I were still working full-time jobs and long hours became the norm for our family. Our daughter Jocelyn was on point as the on-site manager. If anyone is responsible for our success in business, without a doubt, it is Jocelyn. It was her vision that started the journey from the very beginning, and her commitment, leadership and incredible work ethic that secured it. She remains the heartbeat of our business success to this day.

One of the most attractive things about a franchised model business is the fact that you don't have to necessarily be the expert to get started. Not only is there a business model to follow but, depending on the model, a system of support to help navigate the myriad of unknowns that can appear, despite being a duplicated model. Maximizing the value of this highly valuable support team begins with a willingness to remain teachable in every phase. With a genuinely humble and generous approach to helping the team that serves you, comes the benefit of them giving you their very best support, whether it be the corporate support team, your staff and even your customers. The franchise support team will go above and beyond to help find answers to potential problems you may face simply because you take a genuine interest in their success. We have been fortunate to glean invaluable business acumen from businesses around the country due to alliances we've fostered with both area development and corporate support teams.

From our staff, we learn daily on how to better streamline operations as well as solicit recommendations on better safety procedures and training initiatives. Our customers, likewise, play a pivotal role in our growth strategy and the more we voluntarily solicit their input and act on their suggestions, the more they themselves take a personal interest in our long-term success for the community. Consequently, many of our customers proudly claim our business as their own, the ultimate honor of servitude one could ever expect. By remaining teachable we readily accept the fact that we never stop learning for as John Wooten is quoted as saying, "When it comes to learning, once you think you're though, you're through." Always remember that as my long-time mentor and friend Mike Gold would always say, "The best way to walk through a mine field is to follow somebody!" Stay Teachable.

Anyone with a winning thought process must have integrity. They take great pride in paying the full price for their success with no shortcuts. Having integrity does not mean being void of mistakes or miscues. The difference is they face mistakes head own when they occur and for doing so achieve something even greater, trustworthiness. In our business, there is no greater trait than integrity. We learn from mistakes constantly, but we win continually when staff take personal responsibility for incidents when they occur. The interesting thing is that when one staff member acts with integrity, it becomes contagious and all members soon follow. Emphasize from the onset the importance of integrity and you will find success on a faster and greater scale. I remember listening to John Maxwell tell the story of a great policy document used by a very successful company consisted of only two statements. The first simply read, "Do the right thing." The second, "Always remember to refer back to number one!" Maintain a winning culture centered on integrity. Be good for your word in all your dealings and watch those in your corner follow suit.

"Be more concerned with your character than your reputation, because your character is what you really

are, while your reputation is merely what others think you are." ~ John Wooten

There's no chance of success without a strong moral character which embodies the values mentioned previously of honesty, integrity, loyalty, morality and valor. Simply put, your character represents your willingness to do the right thing by others without the need to be held accountable to do so. We all maintain a moral compass that guides us between what's right or wrong, good or bad, and this compass governs our innermost thoughts and emotions when it comes to doing the right thing. To win on any significant level requires character anchored in being trustworthy and transparent. Anyone deficiency in character will have difficulty dealing with others emotionally and most times because they will have difficulty dealing with themselves. If we follow the recommendation of Polonius, "This above all: to thine own self be true, and it must follow, as the night the day, thou canst not then be false to any man," a strong moral character will surely follow. Doing the right thing is the right thing to do!

Maximizing a winning thought process also requires self-discipline that will enable you to overcome success-inhibiting weaknesses. In Napoleon Hill's book, *The Master Key to Riches*, he discusses the existence of the "Cosmic Habit Force" which, once created, can only be replaced by the creation of a new habit. The gap between the old and new habit is secured using discipline.

A winning thought process also contains a level of devotion. Deeper than dedication, if you're devoted to your dreams and goals, there's an emotional connection attached. If you're devoted to the accomplishment of your goal, not only do you want to achieve it, but you love the process and the journey along the way. It's one thing to study music because it can bring riches and fame; however, devoted musicians throughout history proved their passion was far deeper and greater than notoriety or compensation. Their love for what they accomplished was the driver and because of their devotion to it, fame followed. If you love what you do and can also be compensated for doing it, then you are successful and free.

Loyalty. A winning thought process would not be complete without it. Someone who's loyal to a cause or dream has a tremendous amount of allegiance or staying power to see it through. "There's no demonstration or example of loyalty known to mankind better than that of Man's or Woman's Best Friend." – the phrase first recorded by Frederick the Great of Prussia. Two prime examples in our family are Buddy (our Cocker Spaniel) and Blu (Jocelyn's American Staffordshire Terrier). Buddy is 10-years old with a relaxed personality and easy-going demeanor. Blu, on the other hand, is a 1-year-old power terrier who is full of energy and curious about everything. Both are complete opposites. Blu's strong like steel while Buddy's gentle like velvet; yet, both are equal in degrees of loyalty. Neither Blu nor Buddy like to be alone, and they will do whatever it takes to ensure we know that they want to be in the same room we're in. Blu has a rugged, all out temperament and personality, while Buddy has a cautious and timid demeanor. Just like both demonstrate their loyalty to their owners, you must commit to the same degree of loyalty to your dreams. Make you, and your dreams, the priority by being loyal to yourself. You're worth it.

There's very little difference between the hero and the coward. They both feel fear but the hero proceeds despite the fear. Likewise, you can only demonstrate courage if fear is present. Always remember that fear and faith cannot co-exist in the same heart. The winning thought process of success acknowledges the presence of fear, then continues forward with confidence and courage. With confidence, you become bullet-proof emotionally to succeed. In his book, *The Go-Getter*, Author Peter B. Kyne writes about a young man who returned from the war in search for a job and, despite being an underdog, unqualified and having physical disabilities, his desire to succeed overcame all his so-called challenges. With no seemingly chance of success, he willed himself to win. That's what you must do! Embrace the full cost of what it will take to get what you want in life, whether it be time, money, or experience, and pay the full price. While you may be considered an underdog by some, know that there's a go-getter in you and no one can stop someone who won't be stopped. Success is a winning thought process.

CHAPTER THIRTEEN
The Power of Self-love

We have all heard the saying, "It's better to give than receive", but we never give it much thought. When it comes to the power of self-love, however, giving is by far most important. Throughout my naval career, I noticed that within our military culture timely recognition of our great service men and women was one of the most valuable components to ensuring superior performance and high morale. From a Certificate of Appreciation for participating in a local community food drive to the prestigious Purple Heart, recognition is critical to the good order, discipline, and overall well-being the military relies on each day. The countless medals, awards and citations issued are all in response to something significant these valiant warriors had to first give before receiving. Some may have given more than others; however, the fact remains that because they give we all enjoy freedoms no other country has ever known.

It's true: we all have a desire to be recognized, and the desire is so strong that it is greater than riches or fear. There is nothing like hearing someone acknowledge a job well done. This recognition stems from our basic love of self. It's a personal desire that must be satisfied. In Robert Schuller's book, *Self-Love*, he mentions that we are generally motivated by a selfish motive when we give. "Each time we give," Schuller acknowledges, "we do so out of the desire for the feeling of satisfaction and joy we receive from our giving." This desire is not limited to social economic status, wealth or power. It is a necessity that every one of us has need of, whether famous or unknown. We all have a desire to be somebody and make a difference in some way. The feeling we get when we give is so powerful that it must be satisfied at all costs. For instance, there are countless of examples in which professional athletes who earn millions remain unfulfilled, still seeking to win a championship and recognition of their accomplishment by the whole world. It is, essentially, a confirmation that says, "You did good, and you matter."

How much we give and when are also noteworthy. It can largely depend on how much capacity we think we have. When we believe there is abundance, we tend to give more freely and more frequently than when we think resources are scarce. Think of the people you know who remind you of someone with a generous spirit. They always seem to be in a giving mode. They volunteer their time, and their money for the betterment of something or someone else. Considering our natural human instinct for self-preservation first, it is fair to say we have already checked our internal inventory to make sure we have the capacity above and beyond what we need ourselves before we give. That said, even this logical assumption is no comparison when dealing with the power of self-love. The desire for that feeling of satisfaction because of our giving can be so strong that we may even sacrifice our own well-being to receive the benefit of that feeling.

Parents are a perfect example of self-love power. We love our children and any parent would admit that, at times, they go above and beyond normal decision-making for the satisfaction and joy of seeing their children happy. Many parents would easily sacrifice their life's savings to help their kids get into college or experience new lands and travel, when the parents themselves could have easily been traveling.

Understanding how strong our desire for recognition is inside of us, it stands to reason that if we have more, we would easily give more. Very few wealthy people purchase a 15-room mansion with club house and swimming pools just so they can say they have a lot of stuff. Most purchase such things because they envision sharing them with the people or causes they care about. If a dog-lover had millions of dollars and a dream of saving dogs, they would probably buy a farm or facility to save as many as they could. Everyone desires to live a life of significance. Contrary to popular belief, thinking of yourself is not a bad thing. It is a normal thought process. Remember we are ten thousand times more interested in ourselves than in others. Once we focus on satisfying our own needs, then can we can then focus on the needs of others with integrity. Be willing to focus on you first for once.

Ever notice how our mind is always giving us information without being asked? It talks to us all the time. During my idle moments, I'm constantly thinking about either what I plan to do or what I've done. The only time my mind doesn't speak is when I'm in action-mode, doing something at that moment. Even then, I believe my mind is speaking but I am not able to identify what it's saying in that instance. We never stop thinking about ourselves, and that's a good thing because everyone else is thinking of themselves, too. It's amazing how much effort and concern we put into thinking what others are thinking of us, and they're most likely are thinking of you very little. Remember, their minds are speaking to them just as much as yours is thinking of you. By accepting this observation as fact, we can be liberated from the constant worry of what others think. How many opportunities may have not been pursued because of what we perceive others will think of our ideas, our goals, our dreams. If anything, I've learned over the years it's the reality that it's your own thoughts that matter most, not others. By focusing on you, everything else takes care of itself. The person who has an idea to start a business or the person looking to make the dean's list in college must both embrace the fact that they will be in the minority of people to reach those respective levels of success. The good news is that everyone has the same opportunity to achieve their goals once they realize that it's their internal power that is the difference. All success or failure in our lives boils down to choices we've made, the sum of which have brought us to the very point we are today. At the writing of this book, for instance, the entire world is overcoming the largest global crisis in the history of the world, the COVID-19 Pandemic.

The pandemic represents the culmination of a series of choices to either act or failure to act that has changed our way of life forever. The primary mitigation strategy for this deadly virus, to date, is wearing a mask and social distancing from one another, thereby minimizing the potential of spread. To do so, we must first think and focus on ourselves before we can even consider helping anyone else. So, thinking of yourself is a very good thing. It indicates that you place a high premium on you and, once done, it opens the opportunity for you to think of others. For most of us, placing our needs above those of others may not be as easy as it seems. We get great satisfaction from helping others, as discussed earlier. The challenge comes when we must put our needs first to give as we would like. Consider a parent and child flying from New York to Los Angeles. Before takeoff, the flight attendant will brief all passengers on the safety precautions. One of the key directives is what to do should the cabin lose air pressure, and when to don a mask. Parents are reminded to don their mask first, then help their children. The priority remains with the parent to first care for themselves. I don't believe it is possible to give unconditionally, whether it be materially or emotionally, without first being your own priority.

Ask any farmer and they will tell you that the laws of nature do not compromise. To reap a harvest in the summer, the farmer must first sow the seed in the fall. This order does not change under any circumstances. In the King James Bible, it states: "You reap what you sow." If you want to receive generously, it will be in direct proportion to how generously you give. Earl Nightingale in his famed work, *The Strangest Secret*, describes the properties of planting and reaping and what would happen if you planted nightshade, a deadly poison. He reminds us that the earth does not care what we plant, it will give back the same. If you want others to smile and greet you warmly, smile and greet them warmly first. If you want others to admire your accomplishments, admire their accomplishments first. Do your due diligence to make sure you are not giving something you don't want to receive. If you frown at others, you will receive frowns. If you disrespect others, don't be surprised if you are likewise disrespected. We have at our disposal a very powerful ability to set the tone on how our interactions with others will go. Once we give, we should have an expectation to receive in kind, as well. The amount of your giving will also be increased (see Matt: 13:8, KJV "But others fell on good ground and yielded a crop: some a hundredfold, some sixty, some thirty"). So, the good news is that according this law, the return on investment could end up being far greater than the amount invested.

When it comes to how you see yourself, hopefully you see a positive image looking back at you. Whether you see someone who is successful or someone who is a failure is a personal choice. I think we give others far too much credit when it comes to their opinions of whether we are successful or not. The education system for example has well-established parameters in place to evaluate a student's success level but it is far from being all-encompassing. Each time we look in the mirror, we have an opportunity to watch our very own advertisement which promotes our own greatness. Sadly, most of us are more comfortable focusing on our shortcomings rather than our successes. One reason we don't see our positive qualities right away, I believe, is because we are already accustomed to ourselves. We spend all our time with ourselves all the time and, consequently, we are comfortable with what we see and think is our potential for success. The challenge with being comfortable is the fact that we cannot see it all and we cannot see what others may clearly see. For example, I once heard a story of a prominent beauty queen who, despite her beauty, was rarely asked out on a date. She described a large portion of her life as feeling lonely, unwanted and unattractive. When asked to model, she never saw what others could. She had been seeing herself in the mirror her entire life so to her she was normal like everyone else. Once we are accustomed to something we see or do, it is not always easy to see or do otherwise. As the saying goes, "Familiarity breeds contempt." It is important to remember when looking in the mirror, just because you cannot see your full potential for success does not mean it doesn't exist!

Most of us expect to receive positive back when we give positive out. Les Giblin's states in his book, *Skill with People*, that "... we have just a few seconds right before engaging another person to set the mood of the encounter." Considering most of us are attracted to those who agree or are in harmony with us, we can set the tone of the encounter to be a positive one simply by being positive. If someone gives negative energy to another, most times they should expect negative energy in return. Most people don't expect to receive negative after giving positive. This can be a hurtful scenario and the giver may build resentment towards the other person. Feelings of being unappreciated might quickly set in. People and their behaviors, for the most part, are predictable. It's interesting how we sometimes think we know what others are thinking about us. A frown from someone almost immediately translates that they are not interested or do not approve of us. We feel unwanted or not worthy although the other person hasn't even said a word. Yet, we think that they do not approve of who we or what we do simply by their body language or facial expressions. What you will come to find in most of these cases is the other person was not thinking of you at all. Even if they are looking right at you, many times their thoughts can be miles away on something totally unrelated to the moment. Always remember when chasing your dreams that your opinion of you is more important than the opinion others have of you. Once you can convince you, everyone else will fall in line. You are the most important person you know. It's all about you!

Remember, it's ok and necessary to put yourself first when it comes to wanting to pursue the very best for your life. It's not wrong to put yourself first and expect the best life has to offer. No one is more worthy of their dreams than you are. They're your dreams! Don't minimize yourself-worth. You deserve to have the best. I challenge you to hire a new marketing agent for the future you. Up until now, you may have been making decisions based on the opinions and marketing of others. If we endorse those marketing pitches, they have the ability to shape our belief systems, if we're not careful. What if you recruited a new marketing agent for your life? What if you looked in the mirror and started promoting the new you based on your own personal beliefs more than those of others? "I'm going to be the best." "I have what it takes." "I'll be the first to ever do it." "I'm the new line-leader." With this fresh advertising campaign, you'll start to believe you can do more, and you will.

Since success is the by-product of service to others, the more we serve others the more successful we'll become. In our business, instead of setting projections for how much sales revenue we plan to generate, our team focuses on how many people we can serve over a given period. While there are several key benchmarks for determining the success of a business, one of the key indicators of ours is sales transactions over sales revenue. Being willing to work harder, serve and talk more to customers, and make more mistakes in the process, your degree of success has no choice but to increase. Thinking successfully is not by accident, and you should never apologize for serving more. Where your service goes, so goes your success. Be willing to serve on such a level that you're the considered the only one by those you serve.

A spirit of generosity will always be a necessity for anyone looking to serve. It brings with it a message of kindness that lasts a lifetime. When I was around the ages of 8 or 9, when it was a very big deal if you had a quarter. Potato chips were a nickel, and with one dime, you could buy coconut cookies from Mr. Jones' corner store at a whopping price of two for a penny. Any kid would tell you that if you had the chance between choosing a candy bar or the cookies with your quarter, you would easily choose the cookies. Why? You got more. Fifty cookies for a quarter was the going rate, and no child on earth would argue against my choice. I remember watching Mr. Jones reach into this massive cookie jar on his counter with a napkin and count out the cookies as he placed them in a brown paper bag: "Two, four, six ...", he counted out 50 cookies and just before he folded it close to give to me, he would do something I never forgot. He added two more! Two free cookies to a young poor boy who lived with his mother and four young siblings on a dead-end-street was like Christmas morning! Mr. Jones was an old guy who complained about almost everything, but the one thing I learned from him was to give more than what is expected. He taught me how to be generous, and even if it was not intentional,

I received the message loud and clear. Be willing to give a little bit more in everything you do!

I also discovered that we tend to think of generosity as something that is optional. We think we have a choice whether to exercise it or not when we don't. There is a price for not exercising generosity much greater than whatever the cost of exercising it might be. When someone is genuinely generous, people admire and remember just as I remember Mr. Jones Likewise, when someone chooses not to be generous people also remember them but in a negative light. When we add a little extra to our customers, whether remaking a smoothie or providing a Buy One Get One Free coupon, it pays long-term dividends by way of multiple visits and word-of-mouth endorsements to family, friends and relatives. There lies in all of us a spirit of genuine generosity. It is an endless inventory waiting to be tapped into by you, for you.

Confidence is defined as "a feeling of self-assurance"; whereby, arrogance refers to "an attitude of superiority manifested in an overbearing manner".

Achieving success of significance will require a confident – but not arrogant – attitude. You must believe what you feel is possible and take deliberate action in the pursuit of it. For new first-time opportunities, you must think, "I already know I can do it, but I just don't know how yet." Exude a confident attitude without insulting the capabilities of others.

Conversely, the person who displays arrogance intentionally expresses superiority over others, with a demeaning attitude that looks to minimize their confidence and abilities. Bragging would be considered an example of arrogance preying on the confidence of others, with the intent of diminishing their worth, to elevate your own. While different, both confidence and arrogance share some common characteristics and are sometimes misunderstood. Just because a person displays or speaks with confidence doesn't necessarily mean they are arrogant. You can talk about your success and great accomplishments without being perceived as self-serving. Talking about your accomplishments can be of great value when intended to encourage or motivate others through your example. We were very fortunate and blessed to have been able to successfully launch our business four years ago, creating much-needed employment opportunities in the community, as well as, healthier food options. Sharing our start confidently was easy to do, considering it was shared only to encourage and build up others. We are all purpose-driven in some way, and the leader who speaks to inspire does so displaying confidence and unshakable faith.

Be sensitive of the balance necessary to display confidence while being sure not to let the behavior spill over into the arrogant realm. You should never apologize for being confident. It's good to be bold and confident, just not at the expense of others. Successful people master this delicate balance between the two and walk a fine line expertly and you can too.

Even in the darkest of days, we can decide what type of day we're going to have. Others do not have the power to dictate the type of day you will have unless you allow them. You have ultimate authority over it. No matter how dire the circumstances, if you choose to make the day a good one, no one can stop you from having it. You can jumpstart your attitude each day by making a quality decision to control it. I have decided just two options for myself, and only two. I have decided that each day will be either a good day or a great day. Both are personal choices that only I can control. With these two limited options in my arsenal, on my most challenging of days, my day will still be at least a good one. Most are great. When you decide to take control of your attitude, you unleash enough emotional power and influence to take on the world. Make the decision to control your attitude each day by choosing good or great. By doing so, good will be as bad as it gets.

Today, whether you want to start a business, travel the world, become a doctor, launch a non-profit, or buy a dream home, rely on your vision. Trust yourself and go! Accept the fact that you have done an amazing job like no other when it comes to living your life. You are an individual miracle designed for accomplishment and endowed with seeds of greatness, and the world is yours for the taking. You are not here by accident. Your orders are from God and come with all the tools, guidance, and direction necessary for your success. Dreams never die!

About the Author

Clement Troutman is the Founder of The Troutman Alliance, LLC and Owner of Tropical Smoothie Café, Capitol Heights, Maryland, His store has been the franchise chain's top producing café nation-wide for four consecutive years. Troutman retired as an information systems security engineer contractor with the Department of Defense (DoD) after 16 years. A Navy Veteran, he served 23 years in the U.S. Navy, supporting the DoD and national agencies in the field of Cyber Security.

He founded The Troutman Alliance, LLC, which is dedicated to promoting healthier living through the promotion of better eating choices. The Troutman Alliance, LLC established its partnership with Tropical Smoothie Café, LLC, and opened Tropical Smoothie Café, Capitol Heights in February 2017. The café soared from to the number one ranking in annual sales revenue in its first year of operation, and has maintained the spot for four consecutive years with now over 1,000 cafés in the system, nation-wide. A second café is under construction in Vista Gardens West, Bowie, Maryland. Troutman holds a B.S. in Business Management from University of Maryland Global Campus, and is a proud husband and father to his wife, Jacqueline Troutman, and his children, Ashanti, Jocelyn, and Jordan.

www.ingramcontent.com/pod-product-compliance
Lightning Source LLC
Chambersburg PA
CBHW070042120526
44589CB00035B/2258